THE
REVOLUTION
OF
COLOR

THOMAS PATRICK MELADY

THE REVOLUTION

OF
COLOR

General Editor
EDWARD WAKIN

Hawthorn Books, Inc.   Publishers   New York

H-7746

TITLE IN BCL 2nd ED.

TO MY FRIENDS

who have shared with me their
courage, strength and love,
that racial harmony can bring
a glorious sunrise that will burst
forth with the new century

In everlasting appreciation

TPM

PREFACE

In my visits to various parts of the world I have become aware of the increasing importance to the world of the confrontation that is taking place today between men and cultures. My wife and I recently sipped tea with Mauritanian friends on an isolated oasis surrounded by West African Sahara sands. It was a scene of Moorish hospitality that had not changed for centuries. Within a few hours we were in Paris among the throngs on the Champs Elysées. We loved both the tranquillity of the Mauritanian oasis and the thriving dynamism of Paris. Here in simple silhouette is the world of today: men of vastly different backgrounds faced with the possibility of either destroying or embracing each other in the thrilling realization that all mankind can now enjoy the fruits of universal civilization. We are now next-door neighbors and, thanks to modern communications, black, brown, yellow, red and white families, so long separated by vast distances, can now easily visit one another.

Simultaneous with these observations has been the exciting experience of watching the rise to power of the people of color. I have seen at first hand, especially in Africa, people long dominated by foreign powers rise to proclaim their human dignity with a suddenness that history will record as a veritable phenomenon.

I believe that the rise to power of the nonwhite people, coupled with the modern confrontation of men and cultures, offers much inspiration and hope for man as he faces the twenty-first century. During the past several years this has been the subject of lectures I have made across the country—lectures that were designed for general audiences rather than specialized academic audiences because I felt the latter were already aware of these developments.

This book is also designed for the general public. In the following pages I have set forth both the realities and the implications as I see them.

There are friends and associates in Europe, Africa and Asia, as well as in the United States, who have assisted me in obtaining data and in formulating some of my viewpoints. I am also indebted to the audiences to whom I have lectured for the generosity of their comments. To these friends, associates and others, some of whose names I never knew, go my warmest thanks.

There are several friends who gave me extraordinary assistance in the preparation of this book and I would like to acknowledge these services here:

> Lawrence A. Marinelli, who was my graduate assistant at St. John's University, for his thorough research work. I am also indebted to the university administration for freeing Mr. Marinelli from other assignments to undertake this.

Edward Wakin for his careful reading of the manuscript and his precise editorial recommendations.

My wife Margaret has been at my side throughout the preparation of this manuscript. I have depended on her for her
assistance in obtaining statistics, for typing and proofreading
and, of even greater importance, for her constant encouragement to pursue my conversations with others concerning the
facts and the implications of the Revolution of Color.

Without the help of friends this work would never have
come into existence. This book includes both facts and judgments. In this regard I accept full responsibility for all the
information set forth, as well as all the judgments that have
been made.

THOMAS PATRICK MELADY

September 1965
New York, New York

CONTENTS

CHAPTER ONE

SHARPEVILLE AND
THE CONGO

Africa and Asia, the two massive population centers of the peoples of color, can become the plateau of reconciliation where man embraces man, or the scene of the world's greatest bloodbath. It is in Africa and Asia that hope for one world in harmony can become a reality as man approaches the year 2000, or it can perish in the bloodshed of racism. But the confrontation with these alternatives is not limited by geography; it is a worldwide confrontation between white and nonwhite. It is the "Revolution of Color."

This revolution has its roots in the catastrophic misunderstandings of the past between white and nonwhite. Blood has already been shed and the first half of the 1960s saw two significant incidents pregnant with foreboding for the future—the slaughter of blacks by whites in Sharpeville, South Africa, and the rescue of white hostages by white paratroopers in the black man's Congo. These two polar events epitomize the failure of the past, the turmoil of the present and the threat of

13

the future, expressing as they do the emotional and psychological tensions between white and nonwhite.

Certainly these two incidents can be approached from many viewpoints—legal, diplomatic, moral, socioeconomic, political and historical. These avenues would lead into a tangled maze, into the controversial weighing of right and wrong, of legality and illegality, of precedent and prejudice. Putting aside these considerations for the moment, it is possible to examine the Congo rescue and the Sharpeville slaughter in terms of their emotional context.

Approached in terms of their impact on the people of color, they tell an unambiguous story and teach a clear lesson, for they reflect the emotional fallout surrounding the issue of color in the world. While each side may wander into misty logic, the emotional statements of both are emphatic. They enable us to confront the crisis of color in the world within its overwhelmingly emotional dimensions.

Let us begin in Sharpeville on a Monday in March 1960. The aspiring Pan-Africanist Congress of South Africa set the twenty-first of the month as the day for protesting the infamous pass laws imposed on nonwhites in South Africa. Under these laws, an African without a government pass is arrested by the police. The P.A.C. called upon Africans to leave their passes at home on the day of protest and surrender to the police. It was a suitable demonstration of the absurdity, the insanity and the cruelty of the pass laws.

A large crowd of Africans surrounded the Sharpeville police station. They came to be arrested for not having passes. When the police barred the gates, some of the crowd began to throw stones. The police opened fire with sten guns into the crowd of black humanity. The crowd receded like a wave on a beach, leaving hundreds of shoes, trousers and jackets behind—and the bodies of men, women and children, many of them in grotesque positions of death. Two truckloads of corpses were taken away to the mortuary. Some 67 persons were killed and 186 injured.

This horrifying scene was captured in a memorable eyewitness report by a journalist who depicted the surrealistic juxtaposition of gentle protest and vicious response.

The crowd seemed to be loosely gathered around the Saracens (armoured cars) and on the fringes people were walking in and out. The kids were playing. In all there were about 3,000 people. They seemed amiable. Suddenly there was a sharp report from the direction of the police station. There were shrill cries of "izwe lethu" (our land)—women's voices, I thought. The cries came from the police station and I could see a small section of the crowd swirl around the Saracens. Hands went up in the Africanist salute. Then the shooting started. We heard the chatter of a machine gun, then another, then another. There were hundreds of women, some of them laughing. They must have thought the police were firing blanks. One woman was hit about ten yards from our car. Her companion, a young man, went back when she fell. He thought she had stumbled. Then he turned her over and saw that her chest had been shot away. He looked at the blood on his hand and said: "My God, she's gone!"

Hundreds of kids were running, too. One little boy had an old blanket coat, which he held up behind his head, thinking, perhaps, that it might save him from the bullets. Some of the children, hardly as tall as the grass, were leaping like rabbits. Some were shot, too. Still the shooting went on. One of the policemen was standing on top of a Saracen, and it looked as though he was firing his sten gun into the crowd. He was swinging it around in a wide arc from his hip as though he were panning a movie camera. Two other police officers were on the track with him, and it looked as if they were firing pistols. Most of the bodies were strewn on the road running through the field in which we were. One man, who had been lying still, dazedly got to his feet, staggered a few yards, then fell in a heap. A woman sat with her head cupped in her hands. One by one the guns stopped. Before the shooting, I heard no warning to the crowd to disperse. There was no warning volley. When the shooting started it did not stop until there was no living thing in the huge compound in front of the police station. The police have claimed they were in desperate danger because the crowd was stoning them.

Yet only three policemen were reported to have been hit by stones —and more than 200 Africans were shot down. The police also have said that the crowd was armed with "ferocious" weapons which littered the compound after they fled. I saw no weapons, although I looked very carefully, and afterwards studied the photographs of the death scene. While I was there I saw only shoes, hats and a few bicycles left among the bodies. The crowd gave me no reason to feel scared, though I moved among them without any distinguishing mark to protect me, quite obvious with my white skin. I think the police were scared though and I think the crowd knew it.[1]

Sharpeville illustrates the second phase in the march toward freedom of nonwhites in Africa and Asia. It is characterized by growing determination among the nonwhites and fear among the dominant whites, with resulting massacres. In phase one, the African had said, "Yes, Boss," bowed his head compliantly and accepted white domination with docility. Sharpeville can be compared with a demonstration 41 years earlier. That, too, concerned the infamous government passes for nonwhites. Thousands marched to the Johannesburg Pass Office, then sent a deputation to consult with officials before moving on to Von Brandis Square. At the square, protest speakers stressed nonviolence, sending aides among the crowd to collect an enormous number of sticks. They shouted, "Down with the passes," and in the next breath, "No violence." After the speeches, "Rule Britannia" was sung and cheers resounded for the king, the governor-general and Woodrow Wilson. It was in the time of peaceful possibilities.

A native South African white, Professor Edward Roux of the University of Witwatersrand in Johannesburg, who has written sympathetically of the black man's struggle, commented perceptively on this demonstration:

There was no meanness in them but a dignity which might well have made their conquerors ashamed. South Africa may be notorious for the ill-use of her natural assets, but here is the most tragic instance. Of such material as the men of the Von Brandis Square meeting what magnificent citizens might not have been made if justice and magnanimity had been accorded them in place of the prevailing race hatred and intolerance.[2]

But such opportunities were wasted in South Africa, as they were in other pockets of racism throughout the world, and with them opportunities for initiative by the white man. The next phase, epitomized by Sharpeville, was marked by the determination to demand what was not given—freedom and human dignity—but it was still a time of sticks and stones. In the present phase, it is a time of guns and bombs; and in South Africa, as elsewhere where a policy of racial inferiority prevails, it will be the fire next time.

At Sharpeville, the white man massacred the black man and the only answer from the outside world was angry words. After the United Nations condemnations and the demonstrations, the South African racist government stood as solidly as ever. Sharpeville, in the minds of nonwhites, is a contrast with the Congo, where the whites did intervene when the black man threatened the white man. Aside from the arguments of legal validity and diplomatic precedence, an emotional fact remains salient for the nonwhite: it was white against black. This lies behind the strong reactions throughout the world and in the United Nations. Put such arguments aside, in order to demonstrate the highly charged emotional context of the revolution of color. The Congo reactions revealed the gulf between white and nonwhite—the gulf that must be breached.

The Africans bitterly criticized the West's intervention when the Congolese rebels turned on white hostages, for there had been no intervention to stop the slaughter of thousands of Congolese blacks by these same rebels. While the Stanleyville crisis and the rebellion mounted, the rebels threatened 2,000 white hostages, as government forces—led by white mercenaries—advanced on the city. When Belgian paratroopers in U. S. transports began arriving to save the white hostages, the rebels marched some 300 of the hostages into the streets near the monument of the late Patrice Lumumba, the Congo's first premier. The hostages were forced to sit in rows, women and children in front. The soldiers then screamed, "Now we have been attacked, you are going to die." Shooting, and shouting "Ciguya" ("kill" in Swahili), they fired into the crowd of hostages; women and children were their first victims.

The most publicized white victim was a thirty-six-year-old missionary doctor, Paul Earle Carlson of Culver City, California, who for two months had been a pawn of the rebel regime in its negotiations with the United States, Belgium and the legal Congolese government of Premier Moise Tshombe. He had been periodically sentenced to death as an American spy and periodically reprieved. In the end, he died by a cruel whim of fate as he tried to scramble over a wall to safety on that bloody November day.

Dr. Carlson was more than an innocent victim. He was a symbol of idealistic white men and women who have for generations come to Africa to serve the African, rather than to subjugate him. They represent the positive side of the white presence in Africa, but their whiteness became the overpowering factor in the Congo as elsewhere in Africa and Asia, because the white man has also left a cruel heritage of racism.

In the Congo, the black man's bitterness and emotional fury were carried to an extreme, just as the white man's racism is carried to an extreme in South Africa. There was the American Missionary, Joseph Tucker, who was beaten to death in the Congo, one slow blow at a time. It took him nearly an hour to die. There were the five Catholic White Fathers who were dragged to the steps of their Congo mission, stripped of their cassocks and beaten with sticks and bottles. Before they died, they gave each other absolution.

There was the Belgian nun, Sister Anne-Marie Merkens, who described her ordeal after the rebels arrested her, and ended by expressing her will to return and serve the African:

Sometimes in the past two weeks, I wished the Simbas, the Congo rebels, had killed me. Forced to parade naked in the street, my sister nuns and I were beaten till we screamed while Congolese youths danced, jeered and yelled at us. Looking back, I don't hold it against the Congolese, not against the Simbas. They just didn't know any better. For all that I suffered I am keen to get back to the Congo.

After the rebellion had started, Dr. Carlson took his family to safety and returned to the Congo village called "The End of the World" in the native dialect. From that village, where he maintained his medical mission, he wrote of the opportunity afforded his own country: "As God's chosen people for our generation, we have before us the challenge of our world today. The Congo is one of the promised lands. We are deeply grateful for the privilege of serving Him there—grateful and humble for the opportunity given us."

A nun's determination and a doctor's commitment are reminders that in the Congo, in South Africa and throughout Asia and Africa, man's ideals and hopes are not lost. The rancor of racism has not won out, although its bitter fallout is scattered throughout the world.

In the 1960s Sharpeville and the Congo brought out the dangers of racism. They both cast a shadow over the future of man. Signs of racial hate appeared even in the halls of the United Nations in late 1964. Stunned by the sustained outbursts of racism, the late Ambassador Adlai Stevenson on December 14, 1964, repudiated the many sides of racial hate, saying: "Racial strife has cursed the world for too long. I make no defense of the sins of the white race in this respect. But the antidote for white racism is not black racism." The Congo atrocities—moving from black against black to black against white—echoed the madness of Sharpeville in which white victimized black. Racism strikes in all directions, victimizing the innocent, the bystander and even those who try to help—regardless of nationality, color, sex or age. The backdrop for the revolution of color is the grisly outcome that is nightmare to the dream of harmony among many people in one world.

CHAPTER TWO

THE CRUEL ACCIDENT
OF COLOR

Color is a cruel accident that separates the people of the world—perhaps the cruelest of all accidents because it is so meaningless in and of itself and yet leaves such a chasm. It is an accident that is complicated by racial myths and magnified by the misunderstanding of economic, political and spiritual differences. It has built a wall around men and nations, and behind that wall myths of superiority have risen. Being so pervasive, the myths become confused with reality, and man remains securely behind the wall instead of confronting his fellow man. The problem was stated dramatically by Léon Joseph Cardinal Suenens, a wise and enlightened leader of the Catholic church who spoke in accents that are common to all men of good will:

We are still far from the grouping together of people, farther yet from a real communion and from human friendship. Men pass, side by side, as hurried and distracted travelers without exchanging a word, nor a fraternal handshake nor a smile. We do not seek to know what constitutes the profound soul of each people. We do not know the hidden treasures of culture and of noble traditions which could become in the interchange a common good for humanity and an enrichment for all. A first revolution will be made if men learn simply to speak to each other and not only to coexist side by side.[1]

Myths of racial superiority—interwoven with national, religious, social and economic interests—are not new, however consistently destructive they have been to the beholder and the beholden. Among individuals, they can provide self-esteem when normal sources of esteem are lacking, and among nations they provide not only false esteem but also an excuse for subjugation and oppression. The Manchu conquerors of China enforced strict racial segregation and forbade all racial intermarriage. India's insidious caste system grew out of indigenous racial conquests, and its post-independence troubles have been interwoven with agitation by one "subnation" against another. Moslems in India feel oppressed by the Hindus, while Hindus in Pakistan live uneasily side-by-side with Moslems. The Moslems of China's northwest territories revolted periodically until finally ruthlessly repressed in the nineteenth century. In Turkey, the Greek groans, and the Armenian laments past persecutions. In Egypt, native Christian Copts in the Valley of the Nile complain that they are outsiders, although their ancestors were the original Egyptians from whom most of the country's present population is derived.

During World War II, Japanese colonial administrators outdid Western colonial administrators, whom they briefly replaced. Meanwhile, North Americans—who once thought of the Japanese as progressive, intelligent and industrious, under the stress of World War II—readily regarded the same people as cunning and treacherous. Now, just as readily, the Japanese are admired for their skills and their transistor radios. When there was a shortage of Chinese laborers in California, the Chinese were regarded as frugal, sober and law-abiding, but when job competition seemed to threaten the whites, they were looked upon as dirty, repulsive, unassimilable and even dangerous. In India, American soldiers regarded the natives as dirty and uncivilized, while Hindu intellectuals looked down upon the Americans as boorish, materialistic, unintellectual and uncivilized.

This old, old human habit is not only exportable, it grows indigenously. In the greater Antilles, a few years after America was discovered, Spanish explorers sent out investigatory commissions to ascertain whether the natives had souls, while the natives drowned white prisoners in order to determine whether their bodies would decompose. This inability to accept and appreciate human variety is, indeed, a mark of the savage and the primitive. Tribal man, confined to a small area among a small group of likes, regarded even members of a neighboring tribe as less than he, as subhuman, as savage.

Out of this atavistic frame of mind, racial myths have arisen, a patchwork of misconception, fiction and error that have been summed up by anthropologist Juan Comas:

The notion of humanity as being divided into completely separate racial compartments is inaccurate. It is based on false premises, and more particularly on the "blood" theory of heredity which is as false as the old racist theory. Of the blood is a phrase without meaning, since the genes or factors of heredity have no connection whatever with the blood, and are independent elements which not only do not amalgamate but tend to become most sharply differentiated. Heredity is not a fluid transmitted through the blood, nor is it true that the different "bloods" of the progenitors are mixed and combined in their offspring.[2]

The scientifically based racial categories developed by anthropologists undermine popular misconceptions that generalize about superior and inferior races. Social scientists have established beyond any question that there is no scientific basis whatsoever for classifying races according to a scale of relative superiority.

A brilliant dialogue has been conducted in the authoritative UNESCO series of pamphlets, *The Race Question in Modern Science*. A careful reading of these reports and examinations of anthropological findings underlines the complexity of race, and undermines facile generalizations that are more a matter of expedience and prejudice than sober science. In point of fact, national and religious groups rarely coincide with racial populations. The Jews are not a race, but a religious category. The Anglo-Saxons are not a race, but presumed descendants of two tribes, the Angles and the Saxons. There is no Chinese race, though the Chinese are identifiable citizens in many different nations. The Aryans are linguistic rather than racial.

Anthropologists do not agree on exactly how many races there are, though they have developed a working yardstick. To them, the concept of race applies to a socially or geographically isolated population which has come to differ—by frequent inbreeding—from another such population. The differences are measured in certain physical characteristics and the frequency of genes that help to produce these.

It has been customary for anthropologists to divide the human race into three basic groups: Mongoloid, Caucasoid or White, and Negroid, and then make further divisions. A more detailed breakdown of the eleven major races in order of numerical strength would run as follows: Caucasoids, Mongoloids, African Negroids, Melanesians, Micronesians-Polynesians, Congo or Central African Pygmies, Far Eastern Pygmies, Australoids, Bushmen-Hottentots, Ainus (Japanese islanders) and Veddoids (a handful of nonagricultural people in the interior of Ceylon).

One generalization runs through these classifications: all people have the same complexity of brain and central nervous system. This supports the general conclusion that there are no genetically superior or inferior races, although there are differences within the races as well as between them.

Thus far, scientific data is abundant on physical differences, and very limited on mental differences. The end result, as G. M. Morant notes, is a balancing out of strengths and weaknesses that equalizes the races. After noting that group diversity "tends to equalize all peoples when a final summing up is made for all characters," Professor Morant states with scientific optimism: "Variety among populations would be a boon to humanity if all had good opportunities to develop their potentialities." [3]

Such is the careful language of the scientist when he confronts race, as distinct from the racist when he confounds fact and fiction, appearances and reality. For the racist, inequality is absolute and unconditional, one race superior, another inferior, independent of physical, social, economic and historical conditions.

In the context of the present world situation, the dialogue between the races can be reduced to two common denominators: white and nonwhite. It is on this basis that the revolution of color is taking place. It can also be expressed with qualifications as a confrontation between the West and non-West; under these two categories, the problem of the developed and underdeveloped world is subsumed. These equations—West and developed; non-West and underdeveloped—form the bases of misunderstandings that run parallel to those arising from the cruel accident of color.

As Vera Micheles Dean points out, the misunderstanding and the gap between white and nonwhite would arise regardless of communism. It can and does exist and flourish without communism. As Dr. Dean notes, "This is the harsh reality we must face in Asia, the Middle East and Africa if we are not to fall prey to perilous illusions." [4]

The gap between the West and non-West, as well as between white and nonwhite, has roots that are not only historical, diplomatic and dialectical, they are economic, political and spiritual. In economic terms, there is anxiety about aid to which strings are attached, and a feeling that the aid given the East does not compare with the massive aid of the Marshall Plan. Here the West replies that the developed country can absorb more aid more efficiently than the underdeveloped country. Furthermore the yardsticks used in applying aid differ, with the West stressing efficiency and the non-West national dignity. It resembles the difference in approach between banker and welfare worker.

Whereas the West denies intentions to dominate the non-Western world, the memory of colonialism leaves a legacy of suspicion. Then, too, the newly independent countries in their newly developed drive toward power and world influence have their own interplay of national interest and intrigue. The Arabs inveigh against the Israelis, the Pakistanis and Indians still fight over Kashmir, the Turks and Greeks keep Cyprus in a muddle, and the African Continent struggles against Balkanization and displays interference in the internal affairs of other nations. In the political sphere, as in the economic, misunderstanding and mistrust wear two faces.

In the spiritual realm, the emergence of nonwhites in the world has forced the Western world to reexamine its own fundamental values and beliefs and to confront with understanding and awareness the value system of the nonwhite world. The colored races have a renascent confidence in their spiritual values and a determination to maintain them.

The universal values and shared attitudes of the nonwhites are based on the fundamentals of life as experienced by a people whose history has been plagued by poverty, illiteracy and disease. Where life so often hangs by a thread, where fate is fickle and often perverse, men learn acceptance and are constantly reminded of the role of a Supreme Being.

Indeed, acceptance of a Supreme Being is the all-embracing factor permeating the fundamental beliefs of the people of color. The cultures of the Afro-Asian people are spiritually based. In their own way, the black men of the Ivory Coast forest, the brown men of the Sumatra plains, Japanese farmers and Indian peasants of Bolivia have manifested through the centuries—and still do—acceptance of spiritual, nonmaterial values. Simply stated, it is belief in a Supreme Power. He may be designated by different names by Moslems, Buddhists, Hindus, Shintoists, Animists and others, but acceptance of a Supreme Being as a creator of life who rewards and punishes is fundamental to their values.

An interlocking value is firm recognition of primary responsibilities. Starting with the primacy of responsibility to parents, the non-Christian religions have stressed duty to family. Even those societies that still allow polygamy have a strict code of obligations for the man. Of course, there are departures from these norms, as there are in the Christian West, but they persist as abiding standards.

Moreover, the historic pressures of poverty, disease and illiteracy have intensified family relations and extended family commitments of the people of color. In their traditional societies, these lifelong burdens are shared cooperatively and so are the emotions they produce. Birth, marriage and death, the harvest, the rain, the drought—all bring forth a sharing that is manifested in elaborate tribal and family ceremonies.

As in all traditional societies, there is a "festival" mentality among the colored races. It is the most vivid expression of their joy of life, their pleasure in the human activities of sex, sleep, recreation and eating. Deprived of sophisticated, urban pleasures, they confront life in elemental terms, invariably with a spirit of joy. Life is no less sweet for them, because it is so short and so harsh.

Those who have compared the preindustrial societies of Africa and Asia with the industrialized West have been struck by the spontaneous joy that exists in Afro-Asian societies, despite their great poverty.[5] Since a principal goal of society is the pursuit of happiness, the joy and spontaneity in nonwhite societies should appeal to men of good will in the West. It is an atmosphere with which mankind can blend the material comforts of the West. In all their misery, the people of color have maintained a capacity for happiness, a factor that strikes even the most casual observer, who cannot avoid contrasting this mood with that of the affluent society that has lost so much of the spontaneity, warmth and joy of life. This contrast in mood exists in the fact of contrast in living standards. The technological advance of the West has been dramatic and monumental. In modern society, man has been liberated from so many of his ancestors' basic cares and pains that he becomes aware of them only in the Afro-Asian societies. There he sees the drudgery of daily life, the swollen stomachs, thin legs, inflamed eyes and tired bodies. The Afro-Asian man who greets him with a smile will probably be dead at the age of forty!

On their part, the colored races have been influenced by their historic contact with the West. Faced with a primordial struggle for survival, the masses have been indifferent to conflicts in value systems and variations in intellectual traditions. The result has been a mood of accommodation toward other value systems.

For the most part, the Western colonials reenforced the notions of human dignity and individuality, for they at least preached equality and even in practice slowly bridged the gap of inequality. This principle of the white man serves the non-whites throughout the world in supporting their determination to maintain individuality. At least for the nonwhite intellectual, self-respect is confirmed by the Western traditions and ideals he has absorbed.

There is every indication that in most newly independent countries the Africans and Asians are motivated by the desire to "forgive and forget" the superiority attitudes of their former white masters. Thirty-three states in Black Africa alone have become independent since 1957. The tranquillity of this transfer of power was unprecedented, with the exception of the Belgian Congo,[6] where there were special complications. In what other periods of history were alien former masters so well treated by former subordinates?

Clearly, the fundamental compassion of the black people has been demonstrated here. But this mood of "forgive and forget" concerns past attitudes. These people cannot be expected to forgive and forget continuing offenses against their dignity as human beings.

As man rushes to greater technological advances, and as the capability for both human progress and human destruction multiplies, the emergence of the colored races with their power to influence world affairs can add a hopeful note to the future of mankind. On the other hand, racism and myths of racial superiority deny the universal values of the nonwhites and the ideals of mankind. These denials spring from bigoted minds, influenced by ignorance, hate or fear, in defiance of reality and common sense. But more important than pursuing the question of proof is the fact that people of color now have power in world affairs and have crucial contributions to make to the world family. The hope is that mankind will benefit from these universal values, as all men, treating color as an accidental and unimportant difference, face the challenge of living together in the twenty-first century.

CHAPTER THREE

THE OBVIOUS CHOICE

In the mid-nineteenth century, Daniel Manin, the defender of Venice, spoke for all victims of colonialism when he replied to a suggestion that Italy would do better to accept Austrian dominance than to rebel. He replied in what is now a familiar theme as colonialism disappears: "We do not ask that Austria be humane and liberal in Italy—which, after all, would be impossible for her even if she desired; we ask her to get out. We have no concern with her humanity and her liberalism; we wish to be masters in our own house."

In Asia, Rabindranath Tagore expressed the theme this way:

We have seen in our country some brand of tinned food advertised as entirely made and packaged without being touched by hand. This description applies to the governing of India, which is as little touched by the human hand as possible. The governors need not know our language, need not come into personal touch with us except as officials . . . But we, who are governed, are not a mere abstraction. We on our side are individuals with living sensibilities.[1]

30

In Africa, the slogan of Kwame Nkrumah's party in the Gold Coast was also to the point: "We prefer self-government with danger, to servitude in tranquillity." In Guinea, Sekou Toure told President Charles de Gaulle, when his people were faced with the option in September 1958 of maintaining their French tie: "We prefer poverty in freedom, to riches in slavery."

The choice—an obvious one for those rejecting colonialism —has been faced by Asian and African nationalists and set down emphatically: "Better to be governed like hell by ourselves than well by our imperial rulers." Or as stated in more elegant diplomatic language in a United Nations' declaration:

The General Assembly

. . . Convinced that the continued existence of colonialism prevents the development of international economic cooperation, impedes the social, cultural and economic development of dependent peoples and militates against the United Nations ideal of universal peace. . . .

Declares that:
1. The subjection of peoples to alien subjugation, domination and exploitation constitutes a denial of fundamental human rights, is contrary to the Charter of the United Nations and is an impediment to the promotion of world peace and cooperation.
2. All peoples have the right to self-determination.

In the final analysis, colonialism assumes superiority of the white West, inferiority of the nonwhite world. This presumption of superiority characterized the prerevolutionary period in the Revolution of Color and it was expressed in a wide spectrum of domination that ranged from enlightened colonialism to outright slavery. The same theme can be consistently identified—superiority of the white outsider, inferiority of the native. Small wonder that the choice became obvious for the people of color.

The slave trade, the extreme form of white exploitation and domination, devastated the African continent from the sixteenth to the nineteenth centuries. It left deep scars on both whites and blacks and foreshadowed the assumptions and exploitation of the colonialism that followed. Arab slavers operated in the north and east, supplying the Arabian Peninsula, Middle East and Turkey; European slavers supplied the West Indies, the United States and South America. It is conservatively estimated that the Atlantic slave trade cost between 30 and 40 million lives between 1518 and 1865. At least 15 million Africans crossed the Atlantic—the victims of what Malcolm Cowley has called "a forced migration that was more callous, more colorful and immensely larger, in the end, than any other such movement of modern or ancient times." In his introduction to "Black Cargoes," Cowley adds that the distinguishing feature of the slave trade was:

not its dangers, not the loss of life it involved, not even the cruelties it inflicted on millions, but rather the numbness of the traders and their loss of human sympathies. From beginning to end the trade was a denial of any standards except those of profit and loss. A black man was worth exactly what his flesh would bring in the market. If his flesh would bring nothing, he was tossed overboard as if he were a horse with a broken leg.[2]

The brutalizing effects of the slave trade lashed out in many directions. It victimized the white crew as well as the black cargo. Because the sailors were of less value than the slaves, they were often given less food, treated more harshly and frequently had a higher mortality rate than the slaves packed in the hold of the ship. During the days of the slave trade, a Brazilian proverb maintained that it was purgatory for a white man, hell for a Negro, and paradise for a mulatto.

Moreover, few of the slaves were free Africans stolen by the slavers; rather they were purchased from native merchants after hard bargaining. The price was paid in consumer goods and in muskets, which in turn were the means of capturing more slaves, for African tribe attacked African tribe and captured slaves. The result was a state of constant war in West Africa, as the slavers capitalized on the endemic tensions and hostilities.

Ironically, Africa remained independent during the slaving era. The West African tribes, with their courage and skill in using European weapons, were aided by the bitter rivalry among the slavers of various nations. But most of all, it was disease that protected the interior from the Europeans, for whom Africa was a coast, not a continent.

Meanwhile in Asia, colonialism stemmed from the intense activity of European traders, epitomized by the English East India Company and the Dutch East India Company founded in the early 1600s. The Dutch traders concentrated on Java and the Spice Islands, the British on India. They followed in the footsteps of the Portuguese who had virtually dominated the Indian Ocean trade from tiny coast enclaves. The French joined the competition in the 1660s with the Company of the Indies.

In 1818 a climax was reached in India after the English company gained supremacy. As in Africa, domination was accomplished with the cooperation and manipulation of native rulers, as the English outmaneuvered and outfought the French. The English company became a government in fact, controlling all of India. It was not until 1858 that Parliament abolished the company's government of India and placed the country under Crown rule. A secretary of state for India became a member of the British cabinet.

The imperialist race for Africa began seriously in the 1870s and was practically settled by 1898. In that short, intense period, European political power followed economic inroads. The Berlin Conference of 1884-85 set the ground rules for the

European exploitation and carving up of Africa. Britain and France competed for the Sudan; Britain and Germany for the Cameroons. All Africa was the prize and by the beginning of this century the prize was shared by Great Britain, France, Belgium, Italy, Portugal, Spain and Germany.

The domination extended into the mid-twentieth century. Its size and extent seems incredible in the short retrospect of the past decade. Never had so many and so much been in the hands of so few. In the 1950s, the total white European population of Africa was 5 million, compared with 193 million Africans. If the 2.5 million Europeans in South Africa and the 1.6 million in French North Africa were excluded, Africa was in the hands of about a million white Europeans.

The contrast becomes astronomical when the numbers in specific countries are recalled. In the 1950s, Nyasaland had 2.4 million black Africans and only 4,073 white Europeans; in French Togoland, there were 970,983 to 841; in Sierra Leone, 1,776,615 to 598. Nigeria, the largest African country in population with 30 million people, had only 11,750 white Europeans. Even in so-called "white settler" countries like Kenya, there were 5.5 million black Africans and 42,000 whites.

The European presence in the colonial countries was maintained by differing policies. Each European power had a distinctive colonial approach, which varied from place to place. The British used indirect rule, administering through the mechanism of native leaders and operating under an official policy of preparing local populations for self-government within the Commonwealth. In the preindependence era, the British were busily preparing—in stages—for self-government, although complaints were widespread that the stages were too slow.

Ernest Bevin once described the British policy as "Give—and keep." By letting freedom evolve and by developing the native ability to govern, the British aimed at retaining good will and strengthening the Commonwealth. Rather than rule by force indefinitely, the British were committed to national freedom, without losing political and economic advantages. This policy was obviously designed to let the colonized have their cake, while enabling the British to share a part of it. The British could be ethical and also turn a profit for their tight little island.

Within the British colonial empire, there were variations. In the east of Africa, the color bar was marked, particularly in the Rhodesias. In Nigeria, white settlement was forbidden, while in Kenya a white settler minority appropriated the choicest land. But there was always some manifestation of in-direct rule and the intention was expressed by Lord Lugard, architect of this colonial policy, who helped to create both Uganda and Nigeria:

For two or three generations we can show the Negro what we are; then we shall be asked to go away. Then we shall leave the land to those it belongs to, with the feeling that they have better business friends in us than in other white men.

The French colonial goal was assimilation: to take the Afri-can in hand and turn out black Frenchmen. The French did not train for eventual self-government but employed direct rule, which accounts for the large number of French adminis-trative personnel in Africa. During the prewar period in West Africa, the French ruled a population only five-eighths as large as that ruled by the British, but maintained almost three times as many administrators—31,000 to 11,000. The French sought to siphon off nationalist discontent by introducing Afri-cans to French culture and civilization, even sending them to Paris to study. Theoretically, black Africans were citizens of

France—as much a citizen as the baker in Bordeaux or the merchant in Dijon. Moreover, Africans were sent as representatives to the French Parliament. In the 1950s, 52 out of 626 members of the National Assembly and 38 out of 320 senators were Africans. As a result, many of these Africans were more at home in Paris than in Bamako, Dakar or Porto Novo.

By contrast, the Belgians emphasized economic benefits under their rule and withheld political opportunities. No one, not even Belgians, could vote in the Congo. Instead of civil rights there were economic opportunities. Until the end, the Belgians, ruling the Congo from Brussels, were oblivious to the fires of nationalism. A leading spokesman and exponent of the Belgian policy was Pierre Ryckmans, governor-general of the Congo from 1934 until 1947. In 1955, only to be mocked by the events of the 1960s when time ran out on his formula, he wrote:

> If we were to grant political rights in the Congo today, we would have the choice between a competent but restricted electorate and a general but incompetent electorate. Restricting the suffrage to the enlightened would mean handing over power to the European minority, with the risk that it might be used against the interests of the native masses. On the other hand, primitive tribesmen are obviously incapable of recognizing the common good. Extending the suffrage to them could only mean establishing a caricature of democracy and might endanger the future of civilization in Africa.
>
> Such being the situation, nobody in the Congo has been given the right to vote, neither white nor black.[3]

The Portuguese, ignoring both the political and the economic, were more exploitive in Africa than either England or France. Intent on maintaining what has now become an impossible status quo, the Portuguese kept the African in a world of ignorance and isolation. As part of their repressive rule, they provided one innovation: the *assimilado* or *civilizado* system. Under law, an African who passed certain tests be-

came, in effect, a white man as far as Portuguese administrators were concerned. This prestidigitation fooled no one.
As John Gunther has reported, "The catch to the whole system
is that it is difficult almost beyond conception for an African
to qualify." Thus, as a theoretical safety valve for African discontent, it was a cruel fiction. After nearly half a millenium of
involvement in Africa, the Portuguese, according to the 1950
census, had 30,039 *assimilado* Africans out of four million in
Angola, and 4,353 out of 5.7 million in Mozambique.

Following the outbreak of the Angolan rebellion in 1961,
the Portuguese announced a variety of reforms: citizenship for
all indigenous people, and the right to vote provided they paid
their taxes and were literate. Collective bargaining was also
introduced. None of these reforms will change the worldwide
fact that these people wish to govern themselves and will seize
this right if it is not given to them peacefully.

Spain and Germany were comparatively minor actors in
Africa's colonial experience. Evicted from East Africa during
World War I, the Germans left behind some memories of
harsh rule.

In her book *The Colonial Reckoning,* Margery Perham,
the British African expert, cites the labored verse of Sir Francis
Drake commending colonial expansion to his countrymen:

> Their gain shall be the knowledge of our faith,
> And ours such riches as the country hath.

On slavery, Miss Perham comments: "Here, then, in our colonial reckoning, whatever else is uncertain, we can write on the
debit side one unalleviated, questionable, widespread, long
continuing and highly profitable crime." [4]

While Africa suffered from the slave trade, Europe har-
vested enormous economic gains. The merchant shipping of
France, England and the Netherlands benefited from the slave

trade and new industries were provided with markets. Slavery provided primary capital that was invested in mines, railways and cotton mills. And in the Western Hemisphere, the reluctant human cargoes contributed mightily to the settlement of two continents.

Colonial expansion was also a major economic factor in the rise of the West, and with empire came power, prestige and security for the white world. The colonies could provide raw materials for the newly industrialized European countries and, in turn, provide markets for manufactured goods. Meanwhile, their own development could be made subservient and useful to the colonial power. It was a Calvinistic, capitalistic dream as the rich countries became richer and the poor poorer—a brutal and dangerous trend that continues even today. White domination of nonwhites in Asia and Africa—from the moral crime of slavery to the political and economic crime of colonialism—is a study in exploitation.

At the same time, the West planted the seeds for the destruction of its own exploitive presence. Professor Rupert Emerson of Harvard University has suggested, "If it is allowable to impute missions to history, the mission of the characteristic imperialism of the last centuries might be seen as the spreading to the rest of the world of the great revolution that was taking place in the West, a revolution of enlightenment and reason, of science and industry, of the organization of human affairs in war and peace." [5]

As a growing number of native influentials learned the lessons of the West, Asian and African nationalists made the obvious choice: freedom. Many factors worked in their favor. Self-determination became widely accepted, undermining the will of colonial powers to maintain their empires. A general pattern became evident: the more politically advanced and free a colonial power, the more enlightened its colonial posture.

At one extreme there was Great Britain, at the other, Portugal.

Two world wars further undermined colonialism, as the European powers fought and weakened each other. They also depended on the support of their colonial territories, including their manpower. Two hundred thousand Africans fought in World War I; five hundred thousand in World War II. They returned home more assured and more skilled in warfare, the last resort of frustrated nationalism. As the economics of old-fashioned colonialism declined, the burden of maintaining control by force increased. Not only was colonialism immoral, it was becoming uneconomical. Also impossible.

In the logic of current world affairs, it has become axiomatic that once colonial people reach a certain level of development they will not accept alien government even if it is good government. Colonialism brought them to that level and they rejected alien government and demanded self-government. Once set in motion in the more enlightened colonial situations, this wave of independence swept the world, until it is now sweeping away all vestiges of colonialism.

Obviously, throughout the world the perils of freedom have been the choice, rather than the comforts of servitude and domination. Actually, it is more than a choice made by the Western world for itself and exported to the nonwhite world; it is a human choice, in keeping with the dignity of the human family.

CHAPTER FOUR

THE EMERGENCE OF THE REVOLUTION

The rise to power of the people of color is intimately related to the worldwide population explosion. Slightly more than 60 percent of the world's population live in Asia and Africa, the two major locations of colored races. The control of death-dealing diseases, the increase in life expectancy, and the higher birth rate will increase their number to 65 percent within the next decade. When the nonwhites of the Caribbean and South America are added, the scale is tipped even further as the following table reveals:

POPULATION STATISTICS:[1] (in millions)

Area	1950	1960	1970	*(Estimated)* 2000
World	2,500	2,920	3,500	6,280
Africa	199	237	294	517
North Africa	43	53	67	147

POPULATION STATISTICS: (in millions)

		(Estimated)	
Sub-Sahara	156	185	227	370
North America	168	197	225	312
Latin America	163	206	265	592
Asia (excluding USSR and Japan)	1,296	1,524	1,870	3,717
Japan and Ryukyu Islands	84	96	110	153
Europe (excluding USSR)	393	424	457	568
Northern and Western Europe	133	140	148	180
Central Europe	128	140	151	183
Southern Europe	132	144	158	206
Oceania	13.2	16.3	19.4	29.3
Australia and New Zealand	10.2	12.7	14.9	20.8
Pacific Islands	2.9	3.6	4.5	8.6
Soviet Union (both European and Asian parts)	181	215	254	379

WORLD POPULATION BREAKDOWN

(Population Reference Bureau, U.S. Library of Congress; based upon a mid-1963 world population of 3.2 billion.)

Race	Percentage of World's Population
White	31 to 33%
Nonwhite*	67 to 69%

* Approximate nonwhite breakdown is: yellow—31%; brown and red—30% (including Indians, Pakistanis, Malayans, Filipinos and Indonesians); black—8 to 9%.

The accelerated increase of nonwhites in proportion to the world population has been accompanied by the shattering impact of World War II upon the European powers. As Africans and Asians saw their colonial masters brought to the brink of disaster and calling for their support, the notion of absolute white superiority was gone forever from the world.

The worldwide rise and spread of nationalism after World War II set in motion a series of events which have had far-reaching effects on international relations. The impact was strongest in Asia and Africa, with revolutionary effects on social, political and economic structures. Old empires faded away. Power was grasped by the people of color after generations of silence and passivity. An era ended.

In many ways the stage had been set by British, French, Dutch and Belgian colonialism, which opened up wider horizons for their subjects. The West introduced not only concepts of colonial administration, but also liberating philosophical views that were the products of their own histories. The various missionary groups, who until recently had the primary responsibility for education throughout the colonies, contributed to the process. While some of their behavior might have tended to reinforce the notion of white supremacy, their overriding concern was conversion and Christian evangelism. Bible teaching, for instance, introduced the revolutionary idea of the brotherhood of man and the equality of all men before a Supreme Being. Analogies were readily drawn from Old Testament stories about the oppressed but chosen people of Israel and applied to the inequities of colonial domination. Within the Christian framework, Africans and Asians could see themselves as oppressed people destined to find a leader, perhaps a savior, who would lead them to political salvation, which to them meant self-rule.

Furthermore, because the educational program emphasized

European history and institutions, Afro-Asian students absorbed the ideas of the French Revolution and British constitutional history. They came in contact with the "dangerous idea" that it is every man's right to revolt against tyranny; that it is the people's right to participate in the institutions governing them; that government must exist for the good of all the people and not for the few; that there are "inalienable" rights; and, since all men are equal, the same opportunities should be equally available to all. To these ideas, long a part of the European tradition, were added socialist theories of revolutionary action to correct the social evils of economic exploitation. These same socialist ideas held that poverty and unemployment could be abolished and that rewards should be commensurate with work.

The impact of these ideas upon the nonwhite world coincided with the declining power of the colonial nations and the growing acceptance of the idea of self-determination throughout Europe. By the end of World War II, the major colonial powers had seen the collapse of the Far Eastern empires and growing unrest in their African possessions.

In addition, the Western powers were confronted with a contradiction. They had fought two world wars for freedom and democracy, but these same principles had not yet been applied to the colonial peoples. With the loyal participation of their territories, the colonial powers were forced to consider reforms leading toward self-government, if not self-determination.

Meanwhile, World War II had taken a tremendous toll in men, cities, and industries throughout Europe. All available energy was needed for reconstructing a new life out of the ruins. Europe was left without the resources or the will to perpetuate the old colonial system. The decision to introduce reforms was stimulated by the United States, whose traditional

anti-colonial policies had often been at variance with those of
her allies.

Self-determination still had to be interpreted in timetables
and constitutional revisions, which were complicated by the
human, social and economic investments of the West. The
United Nations became the forum for open discussion of these
problems. While the Trusteeship Council had jurisdiction over
only a small portion of Africa's non-self-governing territories,
it was still a platform for self-determination. The council provided the international community with a means of checking
the administration of the trusteeship mandate and debating
each territory's progress toward self-determination. The implications were worldwide and the Soviet Union and other Communist states added to the pressure upon colonial resistance.

Of the remaining old colonial powers, only Portugal has
defied these liberal responses. Her resistance to such drastic
reforms is due partly to her isolation from the liberal European
tradition, and partly to her inability to see herself apart from
her glorious past as a world power. Portugal's national prestige
is tied to her economic dependence upon her overseas territories, and her vested interest in a significant settler community
of Portuguese citizens.

But the seed of rebellion has been sown, if not from within
these territories, certainly from without. The emergence of the
newly independent Asian and African states became a dramatic challenge. They demonstrated that Africans and Asians
can run their own affairs and they demolished the myth of
white supremacy. Of course, doubts about the myth were being raised before World War II, but it was not until the war
itself that the myth was laid to rest. Africans and Asians saw,
for the second time, white man pitted against white man on a
worldwide front. At home and abroad, the cruder pastimes of
soldiers shattered the image of the white man as a paternalistic

colonial administrator. At the same time, African and Asian soldiers fought beside white men shoulder to shoulder, matching them in performance. French-speaking Africans—soldiers and civilians alike—felt the added shock of division within the French government itself. Africans debated the position of Vichy as opposed to the Free French, locating their loyalties with one or the other.

The myth of white supremacy was also demolished by the expanding research of anthropologists and archeologists and the widespread acceptance of their findings. The discovery of buried cities in the Sahara dovetailed with anthropological studies of traditional societies. The anthropologists, concerned with discovering the similarities and differences in human ways of life, helped to show the universal kinship of mankind while revealing the wealth of human diversity. Their studies enabled the nonwhites to see their own traditional societies in a new light, and undermined the cultural provincialism of the white man.

Finally, nationalism in the colonies was fostered by urbanization. Africans and Asians, attracted to the towns, came in ever increasing numbers searching for opportunity and excitement. Once there, changes overtook them. Traditional ties and values were undermined by new desires and relationships. Instead of providing a life exclusively within the tribe and clan, the new towns tended to mix people from a variety of backgrounds and to teach them new skills. Associations were formed on the basis of interests rather than birth, particularly in trade unions and political movements. The new urban dweller counted his wealth in money and bicycles and clothes rather than in cattle or land. He wanted to get ahead, to improve his social and economic position, and he was not content to derive his satisfaction only from the success of his clan. Increasingly, position itself was based on education and job. The urban African became achievement-oriented.

But very often these new goals and aspirations were frustrated by lack of job and educational opportunities. The discontented easily transferred their frustrations to the colonial power and, specifically, to the local colonial administration. Cities in the "settler" countries provided another irritant, for they were divided into native and European areas and the gap in living standards was too dramatic to overlook. Africans and Asians equated white with rich and nonwhite with poor, white with domination and nonwhite with subordination. They grew resentful.

Resentments were easily communicated as were new ideas and techniques for organization and agitation. Afro-Asian newspapers and pamphlets carried provocative stories and seditious statements. Popular leaders harangued crowds with inflammatory slogans and traveled the countryside organizing supporters for demonstrations and rallies. Within a decade after World War II, the people of color became aware of their potential power and were able to translate much of this potential into political action.

The Negro revolution in the United States has paralleled the international revolution of color in many ways. First, there was the breakthrough in the almost complete control of political, social and economic power by the white Anglo-Saxon Protestant majority. In number, too, the American Negroes and other ethnic groups had an impact, not only on the political structure but also on the social and economic fabric.

By the end of World War II, the white Anglo-Saxon Protestant constituency, long the mainstay of political power, was declining in most urban centers. The first to benefit were white non-Anglo-Saxon ethnic groups, while Negro progress was very slow and restricted almost exclusively to the area of legal rights. The anti-segregation decision of the U. S. Supreme Court in 1954 was the culmination of a long series of legal decisions establishing the principle of full legal equality for American Negroes. In the early 1960s, the determination of the American Negro dramatically increased, and by the time of the March on Washington in August 1963 it was evident that the American Negro was just as prepared to fight for his rights as the black man in Africa, the yellow man in Asia and the brown man in Indonesia.

During the Congo debate in the 1964 session of the United Nations, it became clear that the American Negro had succeeded in "internationalizing" his struggle. He had linked the civil rights struggle in the United States with the Africans' charge of racism against the Western World. This was evident in the bitter tone of the Congo debate and the direct references to the American civil rights problem.

The late black nationalist leader, Malcolm X, laid the groundwork for this internationalization and its strategy at the July 1964 meeting of the 33 heads of independent African states in Cairo. He submitted an eight-page memorandum to the conference, which, among other things, said: "Your problems will never be solved until and unless ours are solved. You will never be respected until and unless we are respected. You will never be recognized as free human beings until and unless we are also recognized as human beings." For four months during the summer and autumn of 1964, Malcolm X urged African heads of states in personal meetings to link their own struggle with that of the American Negro. Whether or not they acted directly on his advice, the results paralleled his plea.

An old Western lesson was applied to the nonwhite world: no man is an island. Today, man confronts man as never before; one civilization confronts another. Cultures interpenetrate and societies interact. From the Coke bottle to concepts of the Deity, things and ideas are diffused and distributed at such a breathtaking rate that the world of man is becoming a world of next-door neighbors.

Yet, with the disappearance of physical barriers, psychological problems threaten to keep men apart, for a monumental adjustment faces mankind, particularly Western man. Power is changing hands rapidly and the white people of the world are now only one of three great power centers. They can no longer regard themselves as the center of the world, for the nonwhite people are no longer subservient to white power.

First, there is the traditional Western power group comprising Western Europe and North America. It is reinforced through bilateral relationships between member states and South America, Australia and New Zealand. This power complex is white-dominated, although within it there are diplomatic, strategic and political differences. The Western world no longer speaks with one voice amid the shifting policies of Washington, Paris, London and Bonn.

Second, the Sino-Soviet bloc, relatively new as a power, is rooted in the Soviet Union complex, including the Warsaw Pact states and, tenuously, Communist China. While the divisions and dissensions within this bloc have become more severe than those within the Western power group, there is cohesion in the underlying reality that they are nations imbued with communism.

If we draw two circles around these groupings on the world map, large areas remain outside either circle. These land masses are the African continent and the Asian subcontinent. Some experts would also place Latin America in this third circle.

Before independence began to spread after India became a sovereign state, these areas of the third circle were controlled by the Western powers. The rise to independence and power of the nonwhite people occurred at the same time that the Sino-Soviet complex was challenging Western supremacy. And the threat of mutual annihilation in a nuclear holocaust added a new element to the power structure of the world; total war was no longer feasible. The battle had to be waged with other means in this nuclear standoff.

Yet the West and the Sino-Soviet bloc still carry on their struggle, and the emergence of the areas inhabited by the colored races has created a third force in this contest. The rise to power of the nonwhite people is more than a mere regrouping of the world's power structure. It is the sudden growth of a revolution of expectations among developing nations. Whereas Western man and the Sino-Soviet complex confront each other with capabilities and tendencies to destroy each other, the new third force has dramatically confronted the world with the one alternative to destruction—a new universal civilization. This confounds both the white supremacists and the pessimists. Some regard the decline of Western white power as a terrible tragedy. Others see no alternative but an eventual East-West war that will destroy the world.

The changes in power have enormous implications for the white West. No longer absolute masters of the world, the whites are now a minority group. They face a world profoundly different from that of their fathers. Christianity, essentially a white institution in terms of control, is also challenged. There are fundamental questions to answer: What will be the position of Christianity tomorrow, when the people of color play a leading role in the world? What will future relations be between white and colored peoples? What will be the future of white people in a world dominated by colored people with a non-Western set of values?

As institutions representing exclusively white interests are losing worldwide control, the new world power equation could be the beginning of a new civilization—the civilization of universal man. Will the year 2000—only a few decades away—see a solution based on a blending of Western and Afro-Asian values, where the white man and the colored man willingly merge? That is the transcendental question.

There is some danger that the white man, who was master for so long, will reject this vision of a new society of man. The refusal of the white man to accept the implications of the revolution of color would be disastrous. This folly would result in the exact opposite of a universal civilization: a racial bloodbath that would dwarf all previous struggles in horror.

Mankind at the crossroads has usually recognized its great opportunities. As man faces the year 2000, he has the opportunity to climb to the next plateau: a universal civilization where a full reconciliation can take place between the white man, formerly the master, and the man of color, formerly the subject.

The subject matter, then, is a revolution that may eventually be regarded as the greatest in the history of the world. The significance of this revolution of color, its possibilities and consequences confront a world moving toward the year 2000.

CHAPTER FIVE

DECLINE AND ADJUSTMENT
OF WHITE POWER

The decline of white domination has been followed by a period of adjustment, and, like all unavoidable adjustments, it is painful for some, resisted by a few and accepted by others. The long experience in domination extends from the Hellenistic era to the early NATO period, a historical span in which the dominant whites fought each other for power that was available only to them.

The symbol of the changing power equation is the United Nations. In its early years, it was controlled by the white powers as was the League of Nations, but the change is now obvious. When the 19th General Assembly opened in December 1964, the first black African president—Alex Quaison-Sackey of Ghana—sat at its head, garbed in orange and yellow tribal robes. He was flanked by Secretary-General U Thant and Indian Under Secretary C. V. Narasimhan—an Asian-African triumvirate at the helm of the world organization. They symbolized the rise of nonwhites in the world power structure, an

51

emergence that fills the corridors of the United Nations with a variegated assemblage. This is a reality that predominates in every vote taken by the world body, and figures prominently in every exhortation by Western diplomats—for the West no longer commands. It must try to convince.

The growth of African representation dominates a decade of change. It was signaled by the admission of Libya in 1955 to a world body that had only four African members—Egypt, Ethiopia, Liberia and the Union of South Africa. Then the pace of admission quickened: Sudan, Morocco and Tunisia in 1956, Ghana in 1957, Guinea in 1958, and in 1960—the "Year of Africa"—13 members of the French community were admitted along with the Congo (Leopoldville), Nigeria and Somali. Sierra Leone, Mauritania and Tanganyika were added in 1961; Rwanda, Burundi, Algeria and Uganda in 1962. Then, in 1964, the admission of Malawi and Zambia brought the African representation to 35 member states, the Afro-Asian representation to 53 out of 115 members.

The Bandung Conference of 1955 had been a turning point. Twenty-nine African and Asian nations met in Indonesia, representing 56 percent of the world's population. On this historic occasion, no white nations were invited. The conference expressed faith in "the Bandung spirit" of solidarity of the nonwhite world. Vera Micheles Dean has called it the "land of Bandungia," a land of underdevelopment, of expectations and of nonalignment—a predominantly nonwhite world.

The Western world had to adjust to nonalignment particularly in international diplomacy, to the reality that a majority of mankind was ruled by governments that refused to be taken for granted. While they were not committed to either side in the Cold War, these countries were committed to the United Nations. It is a passing irony that Indonesia, host to the Bandung conference, decided to leave the United Nations. The

fact that Indonesia received no support in this emotional gesture of renunciation underlined the Afro-Asian commitment to
the United Nations.

Historian Arnold Toynbee has recently written:

Africa, then, after the Second World War, seems to be in the
same predicament in which Europe found itself after the Napoleonic
Wars. A high-handed foreign regime has been got rid of, but the
hoped-for liberation has not followed. At least for an all too large
number. Will the map of twentieth-century Africa eventually be
redrawn, as the map of nineteenth-century Europe eventually was?
Will this take fifty years, and will it be brought about eventually by
the application of Bismarck's barbarous treatment with "blood and
iron?" We cannot yet foresee Africa's future. We can, though, feel
sure that, whether her future is going to be peaceful or violent,
happy or unfortunate, she is, in any event, going to count for much,
from now onward, in world affairs.[1]

Self-interest has become a dominant theme for the Afro-
Asian world. The results are a highly selective pattern of reactions to world problems and varied policies. The April 1958
Conference of African States in Ghana expounded the implications of this independent posture in a draft memorandum
which stated: "The time has come for Africa to review the international situation in the light of her own interests. Where it
suits her long-term interest to ally herself with particular countries in Europe, the Western Hemisphere and Asia, she might
come to specific arrangements to safeguard her interests. In all
other matters, it might be prudent and wise to decide her attitude to each issue as it arises in accordance with her interests,
the interests of her friends and allies, her position in the comity
of nations, and the interests of peace and justice."

The adjustment to the decline of white domination ranges
across the spectrum of human activity, from international institutions to fraternal organizations, from religious groups to
private corporations. It was particularly vivid in England and

France, the two great colonial powers of the prewar period. Charles de Gaulle, facing the realities, brought a quick end to France's political empire in Africa and salvaged French interests by establishing a broad cultural Franco-African community where blacks are equal to whites. In the white settler areas of Africa, the United Kingdom was torn by the problem of recognizing the new power of the blacks or protecting the special privileges of the white settlers. As did the French, the English accepted the fact of the decline of white power and responded to the demands of the nonwhites.

The decline had already become evident in Asia. There, the British, French and Dutch empires quickly faded after World War II. In Africa the decline began in North Africa, and in 1957 the end of white rule in black Africa formally began when Ghana became independent.

A similar adjustment confronts Christianity. The Christian Church—whether Catholic, Protestant or Orthodox—remains a predominantly white church and most nonwhite people are not Christians. Within a worldwide context, the Christian Church finds most of its members in areas that are no longer in absolute control of world affairs. This concentration accounts for the 920 million Christians at the end of 1961 in a world population of 2.8 billion, or 32 percent of the total. But Christianity is weakest in Africa and Asia, where Christians constitute about 10 and 2 percent, respectively, of the total population.

The governing bodies of the Christian churches have faced the significance of the rise of the nonwhites and have brought color into the echelons of leadership. But thus far, the admission of black, brown, yellow and red men into Christianity's ruling establishments has not had its full impact. A dramatic gesture of adjustment occurred during the reign of the late Pope John XXIII when Laurean Rugambwa of Tanganyika was designated a cardinal in 1960. It was not until 1939 that the first Negro bishop of sub-Saharan Africa was named. But at the opening of the Vatican Council in October, 1962, there were 61 Negro African archbishops. There are now 74. Moreover, the African secretariat in the Vatican was founded in 1962, enabling Negro prelates to influence the church's decision-making process. By the second and third sessions of the Vatican Council, this sudden and dramatic influence of nonwhites became pronounced.

For their part, Africans and Asians have been influenced by the values of the whites who had dominated them for so long. These values were heavily influenced by Calvin and expressed in the White-Anglo-Saxon-Protestant ethic. The value system placed a high emphasis on material well-being, hard work and thrift. Inherent in this equation was the special importance of the white race.

Against this backdrop, the people of color were regarded as culturally inferior. Students of culture had largely ignored non-Western cultures, which were dismissed as primitive. Attachment by nonwhites to spiritual, nonmaterial values was misinterpreted as cultural backwardness. Their complex social structures and economic systems were often underestimated because of the different cultural forms which they assumed. The myopia of many experts was reflected in the attitudes of colonial administrators.

Consequently the adjustment to nonwhite power must be accompanied by a change in psychological attitudes in the West. As Vera Micheles Dean has pointed out, "It is as if those of us who have been brought up within the orbit of Western civilization—from the Atlantic to the Mediterranean—much as we may know about politics and economics, geography and anthropology, have not yet discovered and explored the inner recesses of the non-Western mind, and are still groping for genuine understanding. We often think of the non-West as an undifferentiated bloc of masses of people. We do not always see the rich diversity of their many faiths, their diverse traditions, their contrasting cultures." [2]

The sudden decline of the preeminence of white Western culture has unnecessarily caused great concern. Those who mistook cultural idiosyncrasies for substantive religious beliefs have perhaps been the most shocked. On the other hand, increasing awareness of universal cultural values has freed those who have not been shackled by provincialism and ethnocentrism. Whites who fear the changes now taking place or, worse still, hate the nonwhites, view the decline of white power as a disaster. Enlightened whites do not fear tomorrow, but rather look forward to a new era for mankind. Which will have greater influence on their fellow whites? Those who fear and hate, or those who love and look to tomorrow as man's greatest opportunity?

The challenge was summarized by the late Dag Hammarskjold when he was questioned about his beliefs: "From scholars and clergymen on my mother's side I inherited a belief that, in the very radical sense of the Gospels, all men are equals as children of God, and should be met and treated by us as our masters in God."

CHAPTER SIX

TRIPARTITE POWER

STRUCTURE

The postwar emergence of the Sino-Soviet bloc and, then, of the Afro-Asians as a third force, was so sudden that the formally dominant bloc of white Western nations is still coming to terms with the new power realities. The accelerated timetable of developments set in motion diplomatic forces, the effects of which remain problematical.

It was only after World War II that communism—first installed in Russia—extended into a series of satellite states in Eastern Europe. When this expansion culminated in the Communist takeover of China in 1950, the West faced a power that challenged its survival. On one side, there was Western Europe and North America, joined by Australia and New Zealand; on the other, the Sino-Soviet bloc built on Marxism.

Then came the Afro-Asian emergence and the casting aside of Western control. The motive power for this emergence was anti-colonialism and the determination of the colored races to rule themselves. To the yellow, brown and black men, colonialism meant not only outside domination, but also domination by people of another color and another culture. Asians and Africans rejected the presumption that they were dominated by superior white people who had a superior culture. They set about charting their own course.

Starting first in Asia, the rise to power of the Afro-Asians developed such momentum that in less than one generation most of the world's nonwhite people became free. The guns of World War II were hardly silent when Indonesia, India and Burma asserted their rights and took over their own destinies. By 1957, Black Africa was engulfed by the same freedom tide. The timetable is breathtaking:

Country	Area (Sq. Km.)	Population	Former Colonial Power	Date of United Nations Membership
ASIA				
(South West)				
Yemen	195,000	5,000,000	United King.	Sept. 30, 1947
Israel	20,700	2,326,000	" "	May 11, 1949
Jordan	96,610	1,690,123	" "	Dec. 14, 1955
Cyprus	9,251	583,000	" "	Sept. 20, 1960
Kuwait	15,540	321,621	" "	May 14, 1963
(South Central)				
India	3,042,794	434,884,939	United King.	Oct. 30, 1945
Afghanistan	650,000	13,800,000	" "	Nov. 19, 1946
Pakistan	946,719	96,558,121	" "	Sept. 30, 1947
Ceylon	65,610	10,167,000	" "	Dec. 14, 1955
Nepal	140,798	9,387,661	" "	Dec. 14, 1955
(South East)				
Philippines	299,681	30,047,000	United States	Oct. 24, 1945
Thailand	514,000	28,000,000		Dec. 16, 1946
Burma	678,033	22,342,000	United King.	April 19, 1948
Indonesia	1,491,564	96,750,000	Netherlands	Sept. 28, 1950*
Cambodia	172,511	5,748,842	France	Dec. 14, 1955
Laos	236,800	1,881,600	France	Dec. 14, 1955
Fed. of Malaya	131,313	7,250,289	United King.	Sept. 17, 1957
(North East)				
Mongolia	1,535,000	998,100		Oct. 27, 1961

* (Indonesia withdrew from membership in March 1965.)

Country	Area (Sq. Km.)	Population	Former Colonial Power	Date of United Nations Membership
AFRICA				
(Northern)				
Libya	1,759,540	1,216,000	Italy	Dec. 14, 1955
Morocco	443,680	11,925,000	France	Nov. 12, 1956
Sudan	2,505,823	12,470,000	United King.	Nov. 12, 1956
Tunisia	125,180	4,254,200	France	Nov. 12, 1956
Somali	637,661	2,030,000	Italy & U.K.	Sept. 20, 1960
Algeria	2,381,741	10,784,269	France	Oct. 8, 1962
(Tropical and Southern)				
Ghana	237,873	6,943,000	United King.	March 8, 1957
Guinea	245,857	3,000,000	France	Dec. 12, 1958
Cameroon	475,442	4,097,000	France	Sept. 20, 1960
Cent. Af. Rep.	617,000	1,227,000	France	Sept. 20, 1960
Chad	1,284,000	2,680,000	France	Sept. 20, 1960
Congo (Br.)	342,000	900,000	France	Sept. 20, 1960
Congo (Le.)	2,345,409	14,797,000	Belgium	Sept. 20, 1960
Dahomey	115,762	2,050,000	France	Sept. 20, 1960
Gabon	267,000	447,880	France	Sept. 20, 1960
Ivory Coast	322,463	3,300,000	France	Sept. 20, 1960
Niger	1,188,794	3,112,000	France	Sept. 20, 1960
Togo	56,600	1,539,000	France	Sept. 20, 1960
Upper Volta	274,200	4,404,200	France	Sept. 20, 1960
Madagascar	595,790	5,577,000	France	Sept. 20, 1960
Senegal	197,161	2,980,000	France	Sept. 28, 1960
Nigeria	923,772	36,473,000	United King.	Oct. 7, 1960
Sierra Leone	72,326	2,450,000	United King.	Sept. 27, 1961
Mauritania	1,085,805	726,616	France	Oct. 27, 1961
Tanganyika	937,061	9,560,400	(UN Mandate U.K. Adm.)	Dec. 14, 1961
Burundi	27,834	2,234,141	(UN Mandate Belgian Adm.)	Sept. 18, 1962
Rwanda	26,338	2,694,749	(UN Mandate Belgian Adm.)	Sept. 18, 1962
Uganda	239,640	6,844,600	United King.	Oct. 25, 1962
Kenya	582,646	7,287,000	United King.	Dec. 16, 1963
Zanzibar[1]	2,642	315,000	United King.	Dec. 1963
Malawi	45,365	2,920,000	United King.	Dec. 1, 1964
Zambia	744,988	3,409,000	United King.	Dec. 1, 1964
LATIN AMERICA				
Jamaica	11,425	1,641,459	United King.	Sept. 18, 1962
Trinidad and Tobago	5,128	859,250	United King.	Sept. 18, 1962

Most of the remaining areas inhabited predominantly by nonwhite people are in southern Africa. There, the timetable has been slowed down. But, inevitably, the revolution of color will extend to the following areas in Africa:

Country	Colonial Power	Present Status
Port. Guinea	Portugal	Overseas Province
Angola	Portugal	" "
Mozambique	Portugal	" "
Southwest Africa	Disputed Mandate Territory now "governed" by Republic of South Africa	
Bechuanaland Basutoland Swaziland	United Kingdom " " " "	Protectorates of U.K. which has recognized their right to self-determination
South. Rhodesia	Self-governing British Colony	Political power actually in the hands of white-settler minority
Republic of South Africa	Independent	All political and economic power held by white minority

Although the people of color have gained freedom, they remain the have-nots. Before independence they had the lowest standard of living in the world, and they still do. But modern communications and the confrontation of man with man have brought the have-nots into contact with the world of the haves. Formerly, they accepted their harsh lot in life; now they realize the possibilities of the affluent society and are demanding a share in it—today, not tomorrow. The revolution of color is also a revolution of expectations.

While the political image of white domination has almost completely changed, the social image remains. Shocking differences in per capita income, material comfort and life expectancy still separate the white man from the colored man.

	Per capita income	Longevity
White Western Europe	$813.00	65
White North America	$2,200.00	68
Black Africa	less than $100.00	40
Yellow and brown Asia	$106.00	51

The life of the white man can be compared to that of the family in the villa on the hill overlooking the colored family below in shantytown. If the white man in the villa does not provide, from his luxuries, some necessities for the shantytown residents, the colored men will eventually attack the house on the hill with vengeance. Only by avoiding such desperate reactions can the aim of universal civilization be achieved and white civilization itself be saved.

The timetable of Communist emergence was just as sudden and dramatic and, indeed, the West was still coping with this phenomenon when the Afro-Asian emergence occurred. Within a few years after World War II, the Soviet Union, which would probably have been defeated without Western aid, became the center of a power bloc that challenged the Western world.

Based on the philosophy of Karl Marx, communism took root in Russia following World War I, struggled throughout the 1920s and 1930s and reeled under the devastating blows of World War II, only to rise dramatically in the postwar period. In one of the most successful political maneuvers in modern history, the Soviet Union rapidly extended its power in eastern Europe and the Far East. The following areas were suddenly added to the Soviet sphere of influence during or after World War II.

Country	Area (Sq. Mi.)	Population	Year of Extension of Soviet Sphere
Lithuania	25,170	2,850,000	August 3, 1940
Latvia	25,590	2,170,000	August 5, 1940
Estonia	17,410	1,235,000	August 6, 1940
Yugoslavia	98,725	18,500,000	November 29, 1945
Albania	11,097	1,625,000	December 2, 1945
Hungary	35,912	9,977,000	February 1, 1946
Bulgaria	42,818	8,100,000	December 15, 1946
Poland	120,733	30,500,000	January 19, 1947
Rumania	91,671	18,500,000	December 30, 1947
Czechoslovakia	49,008	13,900,000	February 25, 1948
East Germany	41,802	17,100,000	October 7, 1949

Along with the postwar extension of Soviet control, communism, assisted by the Soviets, rapidly gained ascendancy in China. By 1950, all of the Chinese mainland was under the effective control of the Chinese Communists, who then extended their power to neighboring territories. Tibet was brought under Chinese control in October 1950. North Korea and North Vietnam also have Communist governments. The following list shows the Asian political entities in the Communist camp.

Country	Area (Sq. Mi.)	Population	Date It Fell under Communist Control
Uzbek SSR	158,160	8,900,000	October 1917
Kazakh SSR	963,815	10,900,000	August 29, 1920
Kirghiz SSR	76,460	2,300,000	April 1921
Turkmen SSR	188,400	1,700,000	October 27, 1924
Tadzhik SSR	55,240	2,200,000	December 5, 1929
North Korea	46,814	11,100,000	August 8, 1945
North Vietnam	63,344	16,200,000	March 6, 1946
Mongolia	604,095	1,015,000	March 31, 1946
China	3,768,100	716,000,000	September 21, 1949
Tibet	470,000	6,000,000	May 23, 1951

The Sino-Soviet bloc now consists of 15 million square miles with an estimated 1.1 billion people. This represents one-fourth of the earth's surface and one-third of the world's population. While the strength of this bloc has been weakened by the tensions between the Soviet Union and Communist China, this complex has played a major role in changing the power groupings in the world. More than any single event, the fall of mainland China in 1950 signaled the end of absolute white Western control of world affairs.

The implications of the new power complex and the role of nonwhites can be dramatized by reducing the world to a tiny village of 100 people. White people would number 31 and nonwhites 69. There would be 33 Christians (23 Catholics, 10 Protestants), while the other 67 would be Jews, Moslems, Buddhists, Hindus, Shintoists and other non-Christians. In this village of 100 there would be 8 Communists and 37 under the domination of Communists.

The white Christians, formerly the absolute rulers, would have set up the social system, but the end of domination by the declining whites in this village of 100 would be apparent. The development of new social structures in the village would therefore be anticipated.

The future relationships in such a village would depend on the ability of the former power holders to accommodate themselves to the social changes taking place. Soon, a black Moslem may become the leader of the local ladies society, the 23 Catholics may have a brown Filipino as their spiritual leader, and the head of the school system may be a Buddhist scholar.

This is the changing shape of the world. Mankind is becoming a small village of next-door neighbors. While the Western white residents are clearly a minority, there is a place for them, as for the followers of Marx. But these two powerful adversaries are outnumbered by the worldwide community of non-

Christian people of color. A hardening of this tripartite division would intensify past animosities and create new ones. The alternative that will enable the residents of such a village and of such a world to live in good relations is the good-neighbor coexistence philosophy of universal pluralism.

CHAPTER SEVEN

THE BATTLE FOR AFRICA

AND ASIA

The death of empire has been followed by a struggle to win the commitment of the colored races, a struggle that is interwoven with their political, social and economic emergence. The newly independent nations have become an arena for the competition between East and West and a choice is demanded, complicating the desire of new nations to follow their own courses.

The Communist goal is unmistakable—worldwide domination. Communist strategy is to make common cause with the aspirations of the Afro-Asian masses and to make them identify their own interests with Marxist socialism. Rather than physical domination in the old colonial sense, the Communists want the Afro-Asians to adopt their ideology.

The Western goal is to encourage the formation of friendly governments or at least governments that are not antagonistic to the Western way of life. Unlike the more rigid Communist approach, Western liberalism allows for a wide spread of differences among friendly states. In the final analysis, the West is well-served when Afro-Asian states avoid policies and actions that undermine their own best interests.

In this competition for the Afro-Asians, the West's main advantage is the root of its cultural heritage—that the dignity of man springs from the existence of a Supreme Being. This fundamental orientation with its primacy for the spiritual destiny of mankind, assures the dignity of man. While there have been deviations from this fundamental premise of Western civilization, it represents the essential substantive difference from a Communist society.

The Afro-Asian cultures are also rooted in belief in a Supreme Being; indeed, in many ways these societies have remained closer to this philosophical orientation than Western society. In the final analysis, the West and the people of color share this bedrock premise, which opposes the Communist rejection of a Supreme Being and the concomitant spiritual dignity of man. The Western man, like the Afro-Asian man, believes in God; the man of Marx does not believe. The difference is basic.

It is this belief in the spiritual dignity of man that provides the common denominator between the colored races and the Western world. Léopold Sédor Senghor, president of Senegal and spokesman for a large number of African intellectuals, has spoken of a marriage of European and African values. In a brilliant statement of this viewpoint before the student body of Fordham University on November 2, 1961, President Senghor said:

I do not bring you anything else except the readiness and the humility of a very ancient people, who have known the vicissitudes of history, but who have never lost faith in themselves and in the future of mankind. This is then the message of our universities of Black Africa, which are a school of life.

To this readiness and humility we have added the method of Europe. This means that we have rejected and that we will continue to reject isolation, even a splendid isolation. We must admit that our relations with Europe have not always been smooth, but these difficulties prove that there has been a contact between two civilizations. It is true also that Europe has destroyed in our countries many values worthy of consideration, but it was in order to bring us other values to replace our own. We have transformed European values into complements of our own, meaning that we have stamped them with the seal of Black Africa.

Nonetheless, the albatross of history hangs upon the neck of the West in the struggle for the ideological commitment of the colored people. The colonial powers were Western. England, France, Belgium and the Netherlands were the heart of the old West. While they, unlike Portugal, eventually yielded power, the historical record of domination left scars on the Afro-Asian mentality. Afro-Asian students by the thousands studied in Western universities and embraced the theories of the great liberal philosophers, then came home to colonies where the West did not practice what it preached philosophically.

France and England, somewhat reluctantly followed by Belgium and the Netherlands, did recognize that time was running out and did initiate policies which provided for a transition of power that was largely free from bloodshed. On this count, the disadvantage is mainly historical memory, but the basic feelings of superiority which permeated the attitudes of Western society still persist. They linger as a nagging affront to Afro-Asian societies.

The man of color is constantly reminded of the superiority feelings and the privileged position of the white man. Although the white man has surrendered political domination in most parts of the world, social and economic domination is evident everywhere. Moreover, the preoccupation of the press in the Afro-Asian countries with discrimination in the Western World reminds the masses that the white man still suppresses the nonwhite. One obvious example is the civil rights struggle in the United States with its widespread repercussions on the press and public opinion of Africa. Nonwhites make common cause with each other in the struggle for equality with new awareness of strength and freedom.

In the Communist bid for the support of Afro-Asians, Russia has led with its political and propaganda battle against colonialism. Associating itself with the aspirations of the "have-nots," the Communists have urged colonial areas to seek first the political kingdom. Whether in the halls of the United Nations or at international youth meetings, the Soviet Union takes a dramatic stand on behalf of liberating the colonial peoples.

Opportunistic, manipulative and hyprocritical, the Soviet approach still has impact. Behind the façade of anti-colonialism, the Soviet Union has developed its own colonial empire through domination of the Eastern European satellite states. Although her ruthless policy of repression was demonstrated by the crushing of the Hungarian revolt, it was Western domination that aroused the ire of the colored man. Attempts to arouse his interest on behalf of the subjugated people of Eastern Europe were unsuccessful.

The Soviets also point to relatively quick success in raising their standard of living by claiming that their system is inherently superior to that of the West, particularly for emerging nations. The people of color, increasingly aware of the vast differences between their living standards and those of most white people, are determined to break the chains of the triple curse of poverty, illiteracy and disease. They regard this struggle as an all-out war and are attracted by the Soviet success story. Nor does the "high cost" in individual freedom under communism undermine its appeal. Instead, the theme "we were just like you" stands out.

Traveling throughout Africa one is consistently reminded of

this fatal attraction. Recently in a West African republic, a Soviet ship carrying equipment and a small group of technicians arrived amid enthusiastic speeches and ceremonial exchanges of gifts. About a half hour later, the young Soviet technicians entered a coffee shop along with several young Africans. The following ensued:

One Russian told the young Africans that he had come to Africa because "we know what it is to be poor and illiterate." In a few dramatic sentences he noted that his parents were illiterate like most Russians of the pre-Communist era and they were also plagued with poverty and disease. He, like most Russians his age, was literate—in fact, a university graduate—and enjoying the benefits of a powerful nation. And all this happened within 40 years. The young man concluded his story by saying, "We know what it is to be poor, ignorant and sickly, and we want to give you the benefit of our way of changing things."

Whether in Asia or Africa, the Communist appeal is to the idealism of aspiring people. Its ugly practices are disguised in high-sounding dialectic. Douglas Hyde, the English expert in combating communism, particularly in Asia, has penetrated the mistaken notions about communism's appeal in the following way:

It is easy enough to say that Chinese join the Communists because they are materialistic, the Indians because they are natural trouble makers, the Indonesians and Malays because they are incurably political and the Filipinos because they are so excitable that anyone can get them to pull out their bolo knives and join in a riot. Quite literally, I have had each of these things said to me at one time or another by Europeans living in Asia. As generalizations they are all equally nonsensical. The Communists of Asia are much the same as Communists throughout the world. In short, most are idealists at heart and in their motivation, but their very idealism has led them into accepting an atheistic creed and a movement which is revolutionary and violent in its thought and action.[1]

Unfortunately for the West, the choice has been oversimplified in Africa and Asia. Capitalism and the West have become synonymous, while socialism has been regarded as a Soviet monopoly. On this count, Western propaganda and narrow-minded approaches to foreign aid have contributed to a simplistic version of free-enterprise capitalism. Too often, the degree of state control and government planning in the West —particularly in Europe—is overlooked. Socialism is compatible with both freedom and democracy, as is dramatically demonstrated in the Scandinavian countries.

In recent years, Israel has helped to clarify the Communist-capitalist choice, for Israel has built a nation out of the desert without laissez-faire capitalism, but with freedom. By sending technicians and aiding in the development of African industry, the Israelis have placed before the underdeveloped countries an example of a free democracy along with a controlled economy. The moral is clear: five-year plans can prosper without brutalizing the population as in Russia and China.

The Israeli example, along with increasing knowledge of the success of Western socialism in the Scandinavian countries, has helped to alter the general impression that socialism is a Communist monopoly. Moreover, the Catholic Church, beginning with the pontificate of the late Pope John XXIII, has carried on an extensive campaign to demonstrate that in Africa and Asia socialism can be a road to economic development—without abandoning respect for the dignity of man.

On the other side of the ledger, Red China's campaign initially strengthened the Communist cause in Africa and Asia. The much heralded "great leap" of China was an attractive example to people looking for economic miracles. The Chinese also added another element to the "we" theme; they spoke as "fellow people of color." This had particular impact upon young intellectuals in the burgeoning Afro-Asian cities.

The honeymoon period was followed by China's economic reverses, its aggressions against India, and a growing fear in some African leaders that Red China looked to the African sub-Sahara as an outlet for surplus population. Moreover, China's nuclear explosion in October 1964 produced mixed reactions and no little apprehension. For example, President Nkrumah of Ghana said that while he "could appreciate and understand the viewpoint of the Chinese people in this matter, we learned with regret" of the nuclear explosion.

By the mid-sixties, the bitter disagreement between Soviet and Chinese communism shattered the unity of the Communist campaign in Africa and forced their sympathizers to take sides or to maintain uneasy contacts with both Communist camps. Communism no longer spoke with one voice in the emerging nations and its appeal was thereby weakened.

While it may be premature to decide whether Soviet or Chinese communism will prevail, a comparison of their two campaigns in Africa reveals significant differences. Both Russia and China approach Africa as an important prize, a continent of new nations emerging from colonialism and still developing their international postures. Many of them are unstable politically and almost all are in desperate need of military and economic aid—conditions ripe for Communist adventures. For instance, a Chinese army document captured early in 1965 called Africa "the center of the struggle between East and West."

Red China's major effort has been to establish diplomatic relations with the new African states. By the end of 1964, eighteen African states had recognized Peking against fifteen recognizing the Formosa regime, with six diplomatic change-overs to Peking occurring in 1964. The two great advantages of the Chinese—as fellow people of color and as a nation closer to Africa in its economic situation than Russia—have been elaborated in a range of tactical moves.

Chinese strategy was epitomized by Premier Chou En-lai's African tour early in 1964. After visiting the United Arab Republic, Algeria, Morocco and Tunisia, Mr. Chou made his first visit to an African country south of the Sahara. He delivered a message in Ghana from the chairman of the Chinese Communist Party, Mao Tse-tung. The theme was familiar: "Imperialists and reactionaries have tried and are trying and will continue to try their utmost to obstruct and undermine the cause of independence and progress of the African peoples." In Mali, this theme was repeated, with the accent on making common cause as Mr. Chou called for Afro-Asian solidarity and "a pact among poor friends." Then he added: "Asia and Africa had the same experience with colonialism. In the days to come, the Chinese people will advance on the side of Mali in the common cause of the fight against imperialism."

However, the Chinese still lack the resources to carry on a full-scale economic and military aid program or to maintain extensive trade relations. Instead, they are waging a selective aid-and-trade campaign. When Peking's vice-minister of foreign trade, Lu Haou-chang, toured Africa in the fall of 1964, he negotiated new loans or trade accords with Kenya, Tanzania and Uganda. Contacts have increased with the opening of Air Pakistan service between African cities and Shanghai, by way of Karachi. A steady trickle of African students and agitators continues to flow into China as the Communist Chinese strive to link forces with nationalist movements.

Limited in their resources, the Chinese often do not insist on sound economic grounds for their loans or grants, as do the Russians. The Russians have, of course, an enormous advantage in the area of military and economic aid as one of the world's two superpowers. They have the resources.

A major Russian disadvantage is identification with the white world, an identification intensified by the furor over discrimination against African students in Moscow. It is a disadvantage increasingly exploited by the Chinese Communists in Africa and Asia as the Russians strive to avoid identification with white colonialism.

The Russian reaction is revealed in a significant article which appeared in the authoritative Soviet magazine, *International Affairs,* in mid-1963. The article, in commenting on the February 1963 African-Asian Solidarity Conference, set forth the dimensions of the Soviet concern by warning against those who "would like to direct the solidarity movement not against imperialist colonialism and its agents, but against all white people." The article also complained of people "with short memories who want to forget that the liberation of Africa would have been inconceivable without the Great October Socialist [Bolshevik] revolution" and warns that in Africa there is "some distrust . . . frankly speaking, of all whites in general."

Whereas both East and West tend to see the struggle in Africa and Asia in ideological terms, it is something else in the emerging countries. They tend to divorce themselves from the ideological aspects of the East-West struggle. For their part, the Afro-Asian states are concentrating on social and economic freedom as an aftermath to political freedom. They shy away from any new form of domination that indirectly replaces colonialism. These young nations are obsessed with a determination to radically improve their living standards. In developing socioeconomic systems that meet their unique needs and respond to their traditions, they are selecting from Western pluralism and communism, accepting, adapting and rejecting from all. The Afro-Asian attitude is against blind acceptance of any single system from the outside. Meanwhile, the aggressive ideological campaigns of both the West and the Communists are having a boomerang effect on many Afro-Asian leaders and young intellectuals. They see overtones of colonial condescension and of superiority feelings and are keenly aware that Asia and Africa need bread, not circuses.

Political analyst Mario Rossi, who has labeled the developing countries as the Third World, has pinpointed their position in the East-West struggle:

In the Third World's present condition, its primary concern—the achievement of viability—is dictated by practical and contingent considerations. It represents an ideal but certainly not an ideology. Ideological involvement would prevent Third World countries from turning to both East and West for the economic and technical assistance required until they can stand on their own feet. It would also make impossible the playing of one participant in the cold war against the other in order to preserve a condition that today affords the Third World a certain sense of security. The paramount reason for ideological rejection, however, is not tied to transient reasons, such as the current transition from decolonialization to independence. Ideologies are divisive and irreconcilable with a world outlook. Consequently, peaceful coexistence cannot be realized except through the rejection of ideologies as instruments of foreign relations.[2]

At this point, a tentative balance sheet can be drawn up on the battle for the support of Africa and Asia. The West's value system, with its recognition of man's spiritual dignity, provides an important basis of dialogue with the Afro-Asian people whose values are spiritual and whose societies are directed toward a Supreme Being. Despite the historical contradictions rooted in the colonial experience, Western pluralism is beginning to awaken a more sympathetic response among Afro-Asian influentials. They recognize pluralism as a system whereby men of strikingly different backgrounds, cultures and creeds can live harmoniously.

On the other hand, the Afro-Asian zeal for rapid social and economic improvement tends to distract them from fundamental values and to direct them toward techniques which will accomplish their goals. For this reason, aspects of the Communist approach to economic development are attractive to most Afro-Asian leaders.

At mid-century the Communists had little or no foothold in Africa, the subcontinent of Asia or in other areas like the Caribbean where large numbers of nonwhite people live. Yet by 1960, this had changed drastically. Besides the physical presence of Communist diplomatic missions, there was the acceptance by various Afro-Asian leaders of the argument that the Communist approach to economic development was the only road to rapid improvement. But this appeal declined as concern grew in Afro-Asian circles about the denial of man's spiritual dignity and the blind obedience inherent in the Communist system.

The main point is that these people resist new as well as old colonialism, but they are ready to enter into meaningful dialogue with all systems and methods. For the West, the challenge is to make common cause with Afro-Asians in the mutual commitment to the dignity of man. From this fraternity, an alliance of great power could emerge to confront the nonbelieving Communist world. The next stage would be a universal civilization in the twenty-first century, in which believing and nonbelieving societies live in peace and where the accident of color no longer separates men.

CHAPTER EIGHT

CHRISTIANITY AND COLOR

Christianity, whose founder was born in Asia and whose Holy Family sought refuge in Africa, is finally facing emotionally, psychologically and theologically in the direction of its geographical origins. In the mid-twentieth century, the Church that went West, drawn by the magnetic force of the Roman Empire that dominated the world at its birth, is facing East—and with pressing interest.

The need to break the narrow Western confines imposed upon Christianity was expressed by the late Pope John XXIII in a message sent in January 1960 to a meeting of the Pax Romana assembly in Manila. This challenge confronts all Christianity, although the message was sent to a Catholic assembly:

Of its very nature Catholicism is universal, worldwide. In the course of centuries, starting from the Near East, the Gospel has been the positive inspiration of living forms of culture which are still bearers of pure religious, moral and intellectual values, and it

76

would be a great shame to discard them. Today it is incumbent on you, among others, to accept the challenge of translating this message of truth and love into forms appropriate to the oriental mind: please realise that we deem this work to be capital for the future of Catholicism.

And in December 1964, another pope—Paul VI—returned from a historic trip to India profoundly affected by his experience. He confronted firsthand the variety of the Asian scene and was cheered by crowds numbering hundreds of thousands and representing half a dozen religions. This was tangible contact with two great realities of the nonwhite world—the great number of people and their commitment to non-Christian religions. On his return to Rome, where layers of protocol insulate him from the outside world, the Pope emphasized that "there is a need for us to produce a more adequate concept of the catholicity of the church."

At present, it is possible to divide the world—with qualifications, of course—into white and Christian or nonwhite and non-Christian. The Christian Church—whether Catholic, Protestant or Orthodox—is a white man's church. The overwhelming majority of the people of color are non-Christian. Thirty-two percent, or 920 million of the world's population is Christian. But their geographical location is predominantly Western, their color white. Next come the Moslems, with 403 million adherents; 292 million in Asia and 84 million in Africa. Confucians, Hindus and Buddhists are next in order of magnitude.

The history of Christianity has been intimately tied to the history of Western man, and thus alienated from the world of nonwhites. After the fall of Rome, Christianity flourished under Charlemagne, dominated Spain and Portugal and set sail with Columbus. The first island in the New World was named San Salvador, symbolic of this Christian predominance. Historically, this has produced alienation from the colored races.

Whiteness permeates the external characteristics of Christianity. Despite the universal mandate of Christ's teachings, his doctrines have been institutionalized within a white context. When Christian missionaries followed white colonialists into the lands of the people of color, they tended to cling to their old cultural contexts and support colonial policies.

In the eighteenth and nineteenth centuries, when nonwhites in Africa and Asia were received into the Christian Church, they were rarely given a position of equality. The blacks, browns and yellows sometimes sat in special pews, received Communion after the whites and were not admitted to holy orders.

The resentment of Africans toward religious colonialism was expressed dramatically in the fall of 1963 by the Most Rev. Raymond-Marie Tchidimbo, archbishop of Conakry, Guinea. His audience was the worldwide assemblage of Catholic bishops and cardinals at the Vatican Council. His statement was direct: "We want only one thing, the pure Gospel. We don't want to be colonials of anyone save Christ."

Whatever the abuses in practice, the mind of the Catholic Church has been clear on the race issue and it can be traced in a revealing chain of official pronouncements, linking the sixteenth and twentieth centuries. Probably the first pronouncement on race matters was made in 1537 by Pope Paul III when he learned that Spanish settlers were enslaving American Indians. In a decree imposing excommunication upon those guilty of such atrocities, the breath of contemporary liberalism was combined with missionary zeal: "Considering that the Indians themselves, though still not received into the bosom of the Church, are not, and must not be, deprived of their freedom or their possessions, since they are men, and therefore capable of faith and salvation, and must not be reduced to slavery but, by preaching and example, exhorted to life. . . ."

More than 400 years later, Pope John XXIII addressed an unprecedented encyclical to "all men of good will"; the audience he sought is significant. In that 1963 encyclical, "Pacem in Terris," he declared:

First among the rules governing relations between political communities is that of truth. But truth requires elimination of every trace of racism, and the consequent recognition of the principle that all States are by nature equal in dignity.

Pope John's successor, Pope Paul VI, echoed this concern in his Christmas message of 1964 when he cited "obstacles which continue to stand in the way of human brotherhood." He indicted racism:

Another obstacle that raises its head again is racism, which separates and opposes the different branches constituting the great human family, resulting in pride, mistrust, exclusivism, discrimination and sometimes even oppression, thus ruining the mutual respect and due esteem which ought to turn the diverse ethnical groups into a peaceful concert of brotherly peoples.

The Catholic bishops in the United States elaborated on this by proclamations on racial harmony. Their August 1963 proclamation opened with a clearcut summary statement:

Nearly five years ago, we the Catholic bishops of the United States, proclaimed with one voice our moral judgment on racial discrimination and segregation. This judgment of November 1958, simply reaffirmed the Catholic position already made explicit in a much earlier statement in 1943.

In the present crisis, we wish to repeat those moral principles and to offer some pastoral suggestions for a Catholic approach to racial harmony.

We insist that "the heart of the race question is moral and religious. It concerns the rights of man and our attitude toward our fellow man . . . Discrimination based on the accidental fact of race or color, and as such injurious to human rights, regardless of personal qualifications or achievements, cannot be reconciled with the truth that God has created all men with equal rights and equal dignity."

Then the bishops tried to drive home the duty of tolerance to the individual Christian:

We can show our Christian charity by a quiet and courageous determination to make the quest for racial harmony a matter of personal involvement.

We must go beyond slogans and generalizations about color, and realize that all of us are human beings, men, women and children, all sharing the same human nature and dignity, with the same desires, hopes and feelings. We should try to know and understand one another.

This pinpoints the crux of the Christian crisis. The tolerance that is basic to Christianity must dominate the attitudes and actions of Christians. Unfortunately, it has not. Most Christian whites see only a white God and a white kingdom of heaven, despite the growing desire on the part of the white church membership to spread the Christian message throughout the world. The underlying superiority attitude of the Christian rank and file sabotages the missionary effort. Until the universal nature of Christianity is thoroughly embraced by its Western adherents, the colored races who now reject white superiority will also reject the religion associated with it. As a result of these attitudes, the overwhelming majority of these people regard Christianity as the white man's religion, and therefore not for them.

The people of color cling to their Moslem, Confucian, Hindu, Buddhist and other faiths that, like Christianity, place a great emphasis on the spirituality of man and on spiritual values. In this respect, the Christian view of man's dignity can be more attractive to most nonwhites than the mechanistic view of Marxist society, as long as white Christians do not persist in undermining the advantage.

The original opportunity for dialogue between Christianity and the great believing cultures of the Afro-Asian world was lost when the first Christian visitors to the Afro-Asian areas ignored the inherent worth of these value systems. However, in recent years an attempt has been made to confront the non-Christian world with understanding and appreciation of their indigenous spiritual values. The basis for an equal dialogue has been established, reflected in the increasing contacts between the intellectual leaders of these great non-Western faiths and the Christian world.

The Protestant churches, especially the Anglican, made the first contemporary attempts to initiate formal contact with non-Christian religious groups. The announcement in 1964 of the establishment of a secretariat at the Vatican for non-Christian faiths added an official Catholic effort to increase this dialogue. In this regard, the annual meeting in early 1965 of the World Council of Churches had considerable significance. The council's 100-man Central Committee met in Enugu, Nigeria.

The response of the Catholic Church has accelerated and is particularly evident in the growing number of Africans raised to the episcopate. The first Negro cardinal, Laurean Cardinal Rugambwa, was followed by a second when, at forty-seven, the Most Rev. Paul Zoungrana, archbishop of Ouagadougou, Upper Volta, was named to the Sacred College of Cardinals in January 1965. The African presence at the Vatican Council achieved formal status at the first session when a new secretariat for the Catholic hierarchy in Africa began functioning in 1962. At that time, there were 300 members of the hierarchy on the African continent, 61 of whom were Negroes.

Their voice was strong and clear on such matters as liturgical reforms. The African bishops received considerable support when they urged that the vernacular languages replace Latin. They argued that if Latin seemed remote in present-day Eu-

rope, it is completely alien to the vast majority of nonwhites.
The contours of the contribution to be made to Christianity
and to Africa by its black adherents was described by Archbishop Jean-Baptiste Zoa of Cameroon in a speech before a
Paris meeting of the Congress of Social Secretariats in May
1963. His concluding statement is a clear definition of the relationship between white and nonwhite Christians:

> Our Church has not to organize things which exist, our Church
> has to form adult Christians, committed Christians who loyally co-
> operate with this Africa in search of itself, with a faith so deep that
> they do not seek labels, that they do without them, accepting com-
> mitments which are supra-confessional. These Christians work
> loyally for this Africa which is seeking its independence and its
> interdependence, that is of an Africa which wants to enter the con-
> cert of nations recognizing interdependence, but with dignity, in a
> way that allows it to give something to the others.

In Algeria, Léon-Etienne Cardinal Duval has personified
the rapport that can be achieved between Christian and non-
Christian. He had the foresight to realize that Algeria would
become free and Moslem-dominated during the 1954-62 Al-
gerian war. Shortsighted French Algerians reacted by scornfully calling him "Mohammed" and terrorists tried to intimi-
date him. The Moslems, in turn, called him their "noble friend"
for speaking out against French terrorism and calling for "fraternal collaboration" in the building of a new nation. With the
emergence of the Moslem state of Algeria, the cardinal—then
an archbishop—was able to establish a harmonious dialogue
between Christianity and Islam. He engineered the Christian
adjustment to resurgent Islamic nationalism. The Church's
schools now play an important role in educating Moslem children; priests, nuns and Catholic laymen help distribute cloth-
ing and surplus American food to Algeria's three million
needy. Thus, when the Vatican honored the prelate by raising
him to cardinal, the government-controlled press heralded the

event enthusiastically. In Moslem Algeria, Christianity has become a welcome friend.

While the dialogue between the intelligentsia and leaders of the great faiths is encouraging, it will only bring whites and nonwhites spiritually closer when the rank and file are involved. Here, the outlook is less encouraging since so many Christians cling to their prejudices. But, as the end of absolute white power becomes more evident, there may be increasing awareness at the grass roots level that the Christian value system is not based on "whiteness," but instead on a universal mandate. On the other hand, many may cling more irrationally than ever to the white Anglo-Saxon accidents of their culture. This unfortunately seems to be the case with the white Christians in South Africa.

In the United States, a promising sign is the fact that Negro clergymen are beginning to appear as pastors in parishes where most of the parishioners are white. In one instance, a predominantly white diocese of a Protestant church in New England is headed by a Negro bishop. In another, the New York Conference of the Methodist Church appointed Negro ministers to key posts as executive secretary of the board of missions and church extension, and as superintendent of the church's Metropolitan District, embracing 57 churches in the New York area.

Moreover, modern communications are helping to establish the universal nature of the Christian Church. The visits of black, brown and yellow churchmen to the white world have dramatized their place in Christianity. American Catholics, who formerly would have seen only European princes of the Church visiting the United States, have recently honored black, yellow and brown cardinals. And all of them possible heirs to the papal throne! Hopes already are rising that the next pope will not be Italian, and it is now likely that by the year 2000 there will be a nonwhite pope.

Thus, various factors are at work. The myths of racial superiority are being undermined by fear and insecurity and also —on the positive side—by enlightenment. There is the growing realization that white domination is at an end and, too, there is the ominous threat of the Marxist power bloc. But, there is the promising possibility that white and nonwhite will be drawn closer by their common acceptance of man's spiritual destiny. From this realization, racial blindness can be cured and equal partnership achieved in the universality of mankind.

But only a few minutes remain before midnight in order to establish the dialogue between the Christian rank and file and the nonwhite, non-Christian millions. Church leaders, as well as intellectual, financial and political leaders within the Chrsitian community, have an obvious responsibility to inspire and motivate their followers and coreligionists. Only the shattering of barriers will solve the problem.

Christianity retains its attraction for the colored races; but it is Christian practice that has repelled them. The overwhelming majority of them will reject Christianity as long as it is tainted with racism. They will refuse to become second-class members of the white man's church or worship a white man's God.

As products of cultures that affirm the existence of a Supreme Being, these people can be drawn toward Christianity. Many can be brought into the Christian fold; all can readily live in harmony with Christianity. But first those Christians who have painted a white God must realize that they are being judged by a universal Deity for whom color is meaningless.

CHAPTER NINE

PHILOSOPHIES OF HATE

Contemporary history has placed a modern accent on the old story of man's inhumanity to man, but twentieth century rationalizations and streamlined techniques fail to conceal primitive emotions and medieval misconceptions. Hate, fear and ignorance reach back in a direct line to the caveman. The rule of force and the role of the half-truth remind us that the age of universal enlightenment has not yet dawned.

Indeed, there is little, if anything, new in the world of oppression; one episode recalls another, one bigot resembles another. South Africa echoes Nazi Germany. A Southern racist in America talks the language of the white settler in Rhodesia. The narrow-minded view of immigration in North America has the same contours as bias against West Indians in the British Isles. Extremists wear white sheets in the American South and they are white men. Mau Mau swear blood oaths in Kenya and they are black men. All are weeds of hatred in the garden of contemporary mankind and they form the context within which the revolution of color is taking place. Indeed, it might be said that the pogroms, the extermination camps, the lynchings and even the lopsided immigration quotas all share the same misconceptions regarding the equality and dignity of all men. They differ in degrees of extremism.

All examples of intolerance depend on identification of the victims and it is one of the challenging ironies of our time that if identification becomes difficult, the oppressors impose it. The Nazis had to resort to pinning the Star of David on Jews, for if visual tests of an Aryan type were imposed, most of the Hitler hierarchy, particularly the mad leader himself, would have failed. However, as color becomes the dominant vehicle of hate, identification of the victim is at its simplest and this very fact of easy identification is a significant aspect of the color revolution. Neither victim nor aggressor can avoid confrontation. A man can change his name, his religion, his passport, his home, his occupation—but not his skin.

Twentieth-century technology has added another factor. The growth of mass media, the development of propaganda, the shrinking of societies psychologically and the growth of mass society mean that bias and hatred can become pervasive and envelop large numbers of people at every level of society. The Nazis demonstrated the point when they infused all levels of German society with their spirit. The respectable man and the man in the street joined the madman on a binge of hatred. When the Nazis pursued the Final Solution (their euphemism for exterminating six million Jews), the pillars of society became partners to the crime. It is a point vividly made by Hannah Arendt in her penetrating analysis of the Eichmann case, particularly when she describes a conference to coordinate efforts to implement the Final Solution:

Although he [Eichmann] had been doing his best right along to help with the Final Solution, he had still harbored some doubts about "such a bloody solution through violence," and these doubts had now been dispelled. "Here now, during this conference, the most prominent people had spoken, the Popes of the Third Reich." Now he could see with his own ears that not only Hitler, not only Heydrich or the "sphinx" Muller, not just the S. S. or the Party, but the elite of the good old Civil Service were vying and fighting with each other for the honor of taking the lead in these "bloody" matters. "At that moment, I sensed a kind of Pontius Pilate feeling, for I felt free of guilt." Who was he to judge? Who was he "to have [his] own thoughts in this matter"? Well, he was neither the first nor the last to be ruined by modesty.[1]

Of the countless examples of the involvement of the ordinary German in this hysteria of hatred, one example in particular makes the point. It was narrated by David Wdowinski, a psychoanalyst who participated in the Warsaw Ghetto uprising. Let it stand as a frightening example of how deep philosophies of hate can reach. Let it stand for what can be seen in South Africa, Southeast Asia or the American South, when one group singles out another as its victim. It is an extreme example for it was a solitary act, free of crowd hysteria, free of outside pressure. It happened as a train of cattle cars filled with Jews was headed for the gas chambers of Treblinka:

Sometimes it happened that a Jewish mother tried to save her child. One such mother pushed her one year old out of the small window onto the grass on a string. She had pinned on the breast of the child a small sack containing a paper on which she had written: "I ask that he who finds my child shall rear him as an honest man. The reward is in the small bag." The bag contained money, jewels, and a legal transfer to a deed to a big house to the finder. A Polish railroad worker found this child. He wanted to take care of it. He hid it in the bosom of his coat. But he was met by a German soldier. "What are you carrying there?" the German asked. The soldier looked at the child, examined him physically and said, "It is a Jew-kid." He took the child by the legs, crushed its skull against the nearest telegraph pole and threw it away. The small bag he took with him.[2]

This single act of brutality not only speaks for itself, but it also demonstrates the brutalizing effect of the philosophy of hate on a single German soldier. Like so many other examples that can be cited, it warns about the beast in all of us, a beast that can brutalize us and our society if philosophies of hate are set loose—and they have been, and still are.

The Nazi nightmare was a shame of first magnitude in this century. It began with the bitter anti-Semitic campaign of the National Socialist Party, a campaign that brought victory, not rejection in Germany's March 1933 elections. More than 39 million Germans went to the polls and 52 percent voted for the National Socialist government. There was then still a choice for Germans and although Hitler meant a variety of things to his German supporters, his philosophy of hate was unmistakable. This alone was reason enough to reject him, but it actually helped elect him.

The repressive policies imposed by the newly elected Nazi government in Germany parallel other policies in other times. The list of measures taken has its echo in South Africa and the American South, for it began as a lesson in the tactics of oppression by legislative and administrative policies. The victim was defined as a non-Aryan, which meant descent from Jewish parents or grandparents; one Jewish parent or grandparent was enough to create a non-Aryan.

The consequences were multiple. Non-Aryans were banned from appointment to official posts in national, state or local government, or from any kind of public or legal corporation. Non-Aryan civil servants were forced to resign unless they had been employed before World War I or had directly participated in that war. Jewish lawyers could not be admitted to the bar, Jewish court clerks and attendants were dismissed, Jewish judges placed "on leave." Jewish university and secondary teachers were dismissed. Tens of thousands of Jewish professional men, businessmen, teachers, writers, musicians, artists and artisans were cut off from their livelihood in this early showing of their hand by the Nazis. There was not even room for an Einstein in a land gone mad with hate. It was a legal prelude and, by comparison with what followed in Germany, only a mild one, with an obvious lesson: hate rushes toward extremes.

Today, the lesson is being repeated in South Africa. Brian Bunting, in his recent book with the self-explanatory title, *The Rise of the South African Reich,* states: "South Africa has not unnaturally replaced Nazi Germany as the fountainhead of inspiration for the world's racist organizations. If the great struggle today is regarded as being, not between Jew and Gentile, but between Black and White, then it is understandable that, in the eyes of fascists the world over, Verwoerd should be seen to have assumed the tattered mantle once worn by Hitler." The observation is unassailable; the outcome in bloodshed, unavoidable.

Just as Nazi Germany labeled Germans "Jews" (having three or four Jewish grandparents) and "hybrids" (having one or two Jewish grandparents), South Africa labels Europeans "Africans" and "Colored" (having mixed racial ancestry). Since some Colored are light enough to pass as whites, identity cards are needed to "protect" the whites. These identity cards also mean access to jobs, homes and schools that are not available to Africans. Thus, racial classification as a Colored means the right to a way of life that is inferior to the white but still superior to the African way of life. The consequences have been devastating, for by a stroke of his pen a South African bureaucrat could demolish the entire position of a Colored family. It is an awesome aspect of racism, for it is a reminder that even limited dignity for the victim becomes an accident of paper work instead of an inalienable right.

But the greatest gap in human dignity is between white or European and native or African. A native is a person "who in fact is or is generally accepted as a member of any aboriginal race or tribe of Africa." A white person is one who "in appearance obviously is or who is generally accepted as a white person, but does not include a person who, although in appearance obviously is a white person, is generally accepted as a colored person."

These racial divisions comprise the foundation on which the shameful house of apartheid or separation has been erected. It has brought about the alienation of man from man. It is manifested under various aspects: biological, territorial, social, educational, economic and political, but its origins were economic in the early part of the century. At that time, the Boer farmers did not proclaim racial superiority, but with the opening of the mines this treacherous policy was set in motion. When African blacks and Boer whites sought unskilled, semiskilled and skilled jobs in the mines, the line of discrimination was clearly drawn.

Enactment of the Mines and Works Amendment Act in 1926 placed discrimination on a formal footing. Nonwhites were barred from certain skilled and semiskilled jobs, and later the restrictions were extended to the building trades. In 1956, under the Industrial Conciliation Act, the Minister of Labor was empowered to restrict any job or job category along racial lines.

As urbanization increased, along with industrialization, restrictions were extended to residence. Legislation compelled nonwhites to live and work in certain areas and their freedom of movement was strictly limited. They were forced to carry passes, and today one out of ten goes to jail each year for violation of these infamous pass regulations.

The pass laws have become a bureaucratic web that entangles, hampers, and degrades the daily life of the African. They govern his employment, his residence, his movements—by day and by night. The urban African is required to carry documents entitling him to a residence in a given location, a lodger's permit, a night pass, a permit even to seek work in a particular area, a service contract, a receipt for a casual labor license or similar occupational certificate, a temporary visitor's permit, a voter's certificate, a permit to attend school and even a pass to exempt the African from carrying a pass. The system of passes became so unwieldy that in 1953 a consolidation took place so that all passes could be incorporated into one "reference" book.

In his account of the South African situation, Edward Roux describes the impact of the pass laws and their degrading context:

The manner of the administration of the pass laws added to the feeling of resentment with which they were regarded by Africans. The rank and file of the police consisted in the main of young Afrikaners recruited from the country districts. Often poorly educated and uncouth, they experienced, no doubt, feelings of inferiority in the more urban environment, for which they obtained psychological compensation by lording it over the blacks. An African travelling about the country or out in the streets after nine in the evening was sure sooner or later to encounter a policeman and to be ordered in no very courteous language to show his pass. Even those few Africans, clergymen and the like, who were exempted from the pass laws, were liable to be accosted in this way. The exemption certificate was in point of fact only another sort of pass to be shown and did not exempt its bearer from the rough demand of the police. In the pass offices, which African workers must visit every month to renew their monthly employment passes, they are often dragooned, shouted at, sworn at and unpleasantly treated. Long queues of Africans are often to be seen at these pass offices. The natives wait patiently sometimes for hours before they receive attention. Any African who attends accompanied by his white employer, however, goes straight to the head of the queue and is dealt with immediately. The writer has seen an African who dared to wear his hat in the pass office have it roughly knocked off by an official, who ordered him back to the end of the queue.[3]

In 1950, as part of its campaign of separation, South Africa passed the Group Areas Act, launching a program of resettling racial groups in restricted areas. Other links in the chain of repression were the Prohibition of Mixed Marriages Act of 1949 and the amendment of the Immorality Act in 1950. Both these acts, in defiance of the beliefs of all major religions and of scientific facts, were designed to "protect the purity of all races."

As South Africa has expanded its policy of forced segregation, more and more laws, definitions and intricate enforcement systems have become necessary. The entire educational system of South Africa reflects these racial doctrines. The government of South Africa has ruled that "native education should be controlled in such a way that it should be in accord with the policy of the State." Since government policy is to keep Africans in an inferior position, the education program follows suit.

What began as discrimination, segregation and separation has evolved into official apartheid. The doctrine of apartheid postulates the complete territorial separation (social, political and economic) of the races. Though the ratio of Europeans to non-Europeans is one to four, many Europeans have been forced into unskilled and semiskilled positions in competition with Africans, but through a variety of devices the European community has preserved its privileged position by barring African economic advancement. Fear that the "European way of life" is threatened by hostile black masses has also meant that African advancement has to be barred politically and socially as well as economically.

The accelerating fanaticism of apartheid advocates is reflected in a statement on Afrikaner nationalism by Professor A. I. Malan:

The whole question of the driving power of nationalism reduces to that of survival. This point is cardinal. He who fails to recognize the fundamental fact that the Afrikaner is fanatically determined to survive as a European race has failed to grasp the most elementary fact of South African politics. Why this fanaticism? Let us consider the facts, and maybe the reason will become clear. The Continent of Africa contains roughly 230,000,000 people of whom 4,000,000 are white, and among these Europeans there is only one single and distinct nation, the Afrikaner nation. For better or for worse this tiny nation has decided that, in spite of the overwhelming preponderance of black and colored races, it is going to survive as the European nation at the southern extremity of Africa. The object of Afrikaner nationalism is primarily the perpetuation of European culture at a limited corner of the vast Continent of Africa . . . The matter of survival has become an irresistible life force, and veritable obsession.

In this obsession, the Afrikaner white draws powerful assistance from his church. Almost one-half of the European population belongs to the Dutch Reform Church, whose Calvinist doctrines have been perverted to sanction white superiority. Isolated by the rest of the Christian churches, this group adds a religious fervor to the clear economic motives for the maintenance of white privilege and domination.

In South Africa today the white minority defies all moral, legal and scientific arguments against its racial superiority doctrines. They blindly insist that they are superior and they will go to any extreme to maintain their special privileges and to deprive nonwhites of their fundamental human rights.

The so-called 90-day law is a case in point. In a piece of legal barbarism reminiscent of the free hand given the Gestapo in Nazi Germany, the government was given the right to put any person in solitary confinement without charge or trial. When the law was suspended late in 1964, the editorial comments in South African newspapers revealed the awareness even in South Africa of its repressive nature. Hate, as in Germany, had rushed toward extremes.

Said the *Johannesburg Star:* "No country which wants to pass as civilized and which attaches any importance to the rule of law can afford to tolerate such a negation of habeas corpus —a denial to the right of the individual which is basic to the democratic way of life."

Said the *Johannesburg Sunday Times* about arguments that the 90-day law had been effective: "But this argument can with equal logic be used to justify even tougher methods—the thumbscrew, the rack and the rubber truncheon. These would presumably be even more effective in getting results."

The *Johannesburg Sunday Express* in a warning heard in other countries at other times cited "the steady drift toward authoritarian rule." It also criticized citizens who were indifferent to arrest under the 90-day law and who consoled themselves with the thought that the victims "must have been up to something." At every turn in South Africa, one is tempted to hold up the story of the rise and fall of the Third Reich.

Meanwhile, the reaction of South African nonwhites toward the oppressive situation is changing. Until a few years ago, they accepted the humiliations of a policy that said: "God made you inferior and we are going to keep you that way." As described in the first chapter, March 21, 1960, marked the end of African passivity. On this day, Africans who were demonstrating peacefully in Sharpeville were told to disperse by the white police. Formerly, they would have obeyed, but this time they continued their demonstration. The police opened fire, killing 67 Africans and wounding many others.

While South African nonwhites have always rejected the inferior label applied by the white government, they have previously expressed this opposition primarily through nonviolent means. But in the face of the violence being directed toward the Africans, nonviolence is quickly changing to violence. The

Africans intend to fight for their rights even in the face of increasingly brutal repressive measures.

South Africa presents the West, particularly the United States, with an acute problem. The elements in the situation are clear. The nonwhites are determined to fight for freedom at any cost. The Sino-Soviet bloc is offering them the support needed for violent action. So are many African nations. Western economic stakes are high in South Africa, as are the moral, ideological and diplomatic stakes.

Time is on the side of the nonwhites in South Africa, and the West is challenged to act before the events rush toward more violent measures. As the South Africa government becomes more oppressive, it provokes even greater violence in a defeat that is inevitable. The desperation in South Africa is brought about by the refusal of the whites there to accept change, to accept progress, to accept reality.

The lesson is obvious. South African whites have sown the seeds of racial inequality and they will reap the destruction. But the consequences will be felt all over the world, unless a concerted, multipronged effort is made to change this direction of events. A sense of urgency is needed in the West and in the United States. A giant effort must be undertaken, for disaster is truly around the corner in South Africa.

However, the struggle against philosophies of hate and intolerance also begins at home and on this count each nation must look within its own house. Black, white and yellow, East and West, the poison is widespread, contaminating its victims as well as those countries leading in the struggle against racism.

Although the United States has boldly confronted the intransigence of the American South, a lesser-known disgrace was only belatedly confronted. It was the anachronistic immigration policy of the United States, embodied in a forty-year-old law. Since 1952, when the McCarran-Walter Immigration and Na-

tionality Act was passed over President Truman's veto, efforts
to liberalize U. S. immigration policies have been thwarted.
The heart of that policy was the national quota system which
President Johnson has called "incompatible with our basic
American tradition" and a source of "incalculable harm." A
key provision has been the "Asia-Pacific triangle" arrangement
which has effectively barred all but a handful of Oriental im-
migrants to the United States—a stubborn hangover of the
"yellow peril" mentality that afflicted America.

On January 14, 1965, *The Reporter* magazine summed up
the indictment of U. S. immigration policy in an authoritative
article:

As a result, critics regard U. S. immigration regulations as a
hodgepodge of rigid and cruel absurdities that flagrantly discrimi-
nate against countries in Southern and Eastern Europe, Asia and
Africa, thereby undermining our foreign-policy objectives. Furthermore, for all its stress on keeping out Communist sympathizers, the
McCarran-Walter Act makes no provision for helping those who
escape from the Soviet orbit. Only through special acts were ref-
ugees from Hungary and Cuba admitted.

Early in 1965, as President Johnson argued against this immigration policy, England confronted a problem with similar
overtones. Rising popular feeling against the influx of immi-
grants from the West Indies, Pakistan and India had become
evident; in the fall of 1964, the Gallup poll found 68 percent
of all Britons in favor of some curbs on immigration. Against
this background, Britain's Labor Party cabinet was deprived
of its Foreign Secretary and almost brought down in a chain of
events that recalls the adage about the loss of a battle for want
of a nail. The nail in this case was racism, a reminder that even
in the heart of parliamentary democracy philosophies of hate
cast a shadow.

This chain of events had begun with the defeat of Gordon
Walker in the fall 1964 parliamentary elections over the race

issue. Smears scrawled on the stone walls of the Smethwick constituency where Walker was running told the ugly story: "If you want a nigger neighbor, vote Labor." The result was a defeat for the man slated to become Britain's Foreign Secretary, as the racially mixed factory town of Smethwick gave way to the fear that the Labor Party would be "soft" on the issue of colored immigration.

In a special by-election to provide Walker with the parliamentary seat, he ran again and lost. Other factors, as well as the race issue, were at work this time, but the ugly reminders remained as British Nazis invaded Walker's first campaign rally. The victim, Gordon Walker, was a farseeing politician who opposed immigration curbs in 1961 by calling such measures "barefaced racial discrimination" and warned of the damage to Britain's Commonwealth partners. In 1964 and 1965 the victim was also the Labor Party and, indeed, the entire country.

Other examples crop up all around the world, even in such unexpected countries as Brazil and Israel. Early in 1965, Israeli Premier Levi Eshkol pointed out a "central problem in our lives"—the gap between the Ashkenazi or European Jews and the Sephardic Jews from Asia and Africa. It was a gap that some regarded as great a threat as the military threat posed by hostile Arab neighbors. While there is no official discrimination in Israel, the Sephardic Jews encounter it in daily living in social and economic manifestations. A derogatory term, "Cushi" (the biblical term for Negro), has emerged with the same perjorative meaning in Israel as "nigger" in the United States.

Brazil, reputed to be a model of racial harmony, was reminded of the depressed lot of its Negroes in an authoritative study made by Professor Florestan Fernandes of the University of São Paulo. His findings run counter to the complacent self-image of Brazilians drawn by President Janio Quadros who said: "We have become the most successful example of racial coexistence and integration known in history." He said this in a country where newspaper ads for jobs and apartments specify "only light-skinned need apply" or, bluntly, "whites only." He said this in a country which is 38 percent Negro and where only 3 percent of the army's officers and none of the air force or navy officers are Negroes. He said this in a country where virtually all the top officials are of European descent. He said this in a country where a few years ago not a single mulatto or Negro diplomat could be found to send to a conference in Africa. He said this in a country which at that time still had only one colored diplomat, a newly chosen ambassador to Algeria. Professor Fernandes summed up the Brazilian situation better than the president when he said: "If we help the Negro get ahead, our democracy will win a major victory. If we fight him as an economic competitor and a threat to white supremacy, we can only bring about anger and bitterness."

Nor can the Iron Curtain conceal racism in the Communist countries, despite their carefully contrived courtship of Asia and Africa. Certainly a climax was reached in the unprecedented riot of December 1963 in Red Square, that symbolic center of agitation. When 500 African students grappled and scuffled with Soviet police, the Soviet façade of tolerance was torn down before the world. A continuing experience with harassment had broken into open protest by the very students who were subsidized by the Russians. They were not biting the white hand that had subsidized them, but the white intolerance that humiliated them.

Racism in Russia was out in the open, but the evidence had been accumulating. A little-known "open letter" presented in September 21, 1960, in Frankfurt, Germany, by three African students who had been enrolled at Moscow State University, states the case in unmistakable terms, as is evident from the following:

> The decision to present the case against communism to African and world opinion was taken in secret executive session in Moscow by representatives from Algeria, the Cameroons, the Congo, Ghana, Guinea, Kenya, Mali, Morocco, Nigeria, Sudan, Togo, Tunisia, UAR and Uganda. Members of the Executive Committee were given the duty of presenting the case when they got out of the Soviet Union.
>
> Our accusations are directed against the Communist rulers, not against the friendly Russian people we met and some of whom we came to love, not against the mother of four who ran out in the streets to welcome African students on a controlled tour and in parting said "Tell your people in Africa that there are more people here to be liberated than in Africa," and not against the Pasternaks, great and small, of Russia who compassionately seek the brotherhood of man. No, we accuse the disastrous ambition of Communist dictatorship and its bureaucracy that have brought terror and fear to much of the world. . . .
>
> We have also observed that the Soviets have not accepted the Chinese, and vice versa, except as political brothers. The many thousands of Chinese here seldom go in the company of the Soviets —they hardly fraternize except in anti-Western gatherings. We fail to see any deeply-rooted feelings in their relations, and what is more, the Chinese know it.

But even the average Russian has not been free of bias toward the African in particular, despite the emphasis on official attitudes in the above indictment. *New York Times* Moscow correspondent Theodore Shabad, in reporting on the situation on December 19, 1963, pointed out that "most Russians have only a confused notion of modern Africa and still picture the 'dark continent' largely in terms of a jungle inhabited by monkeys and half-clothed black men." As correspondent Shabad also points out, problems of sexual jealousy are evident when Africans socialize with Russian girls, particularly when they date them. The widely publicized African student riot in 1963 was in fact precipitated by the mysterious death of a Ghanian medical student who had planned to marry a Russian girl. As one observer of Africans in Moscow has noted, they come expecting a warm welcome and are unpleasantly surprised, while the opposite has occurred in the United States where they expect rebuffs and usually find hospitality.

On the African side, the dark chapter of the Mau Mau shows the extremism that can afflict the nonwhite when racism poisons him. He strikes out against fellow black as well as white and the horror of it all becomes unspeakable. The Mau Mau oath was an oath to kill and it held such promises as:

If I am called upon to do so, with four others I will kill a European.
If I am called upon to do so, I will kill a Kikuyu who is against Mau Mau, even if it be my mother or my father or brother or sister or wife or child.

Just as a single incident—the previously mentioned solitary killing of a Jewish baby by a German soldier—can illustrate the Nazi rampage, the murder of a single six-year-old boy can indicate the ferocity of the Mau Mau episode. It happened on a beguiling starlit Saturday night, January 23, 1953, when the Ruck family were at home on their Kenya farm. There seemed to be no likehood that they would be singled out by the Mau Mau, for they had exemplary attitudes toward the Africans in their area. Mrs. Ruck, a doctor, donated her skills and her services to a clinic that served Africans, and her husband worked the farm.

When the Mau Mau struck, they first lured the husband outdoors and then his wife, killing and mutilating them. Upstairs, six-year-old Michael Ruck began to cry and one of the raiders was sent to silence him. "The official police photograph of Michael Ruck as Mau Mau left him is something unlikely to be surpassed in grievous nauseating horror."[4]

So runs the chilling Odyssey through the twentieth century

chronicle of man's inhumanity to man, a chronicle of blood-shed built on crazed rationalizations and hysterical oaths. And certainly no one evoked the insanity of the rationalizations more completely than Adolf Hitler in *Mein Kampf*. The section "People and Race" bristles with mad syllogisms and demented generalizations, all of them signposts in the direction of un-speakable atrocities:

The stronger must rule; it must not unite with the weaker, thus sacrificing its own stature. Only the born weakling can think this cruel, and that is why he is a weak and defective man; for if this law did not hold, any conceivable evolution of organic living things would be unthinkable.

The great civilizations of the past have all been destroyed simply because the originally creative race died out through blood-poi-soning. . . .

Mingling of blood, with the decline in racial level that it causes, is the sole reason for the dying-out of old cultures; for men are destroyed not by lost wars, but by losing that stamina inherent in pure blood alone. . . .

Lost purity of blood alone destroys inner happiness forever, and lowers man irrevocably; the results can never again be eliminated from body and spirit.

If we examine and compare all the other problems of life as against this one question, we shall come to realize how ridiculously small they are by comparison. They are all temporarily limited—but the question of preserving or not preserving purity of blood will remain so long as there are human beings.

From the pogrom to the biased immigration quota, from the epithet to the gas oven, racism asserts its universality—how-ever it varies in its manifestations. Racism alienates man from man and can destroy mankind. How far, how wide its dimen-sions! How universal, too, the revolution of color! Yet, just as hate rushes to extremes as it poisons, so philosophies of hu-man equality and evidence of harmony act as antidotes. It is these philosophies of hope that belong to the near and prom-ising future.

CHAPTER TEN

PHILOSOPHIES OF HOPE

A nation like its citizens, a civilization like the men in it, a society like its individual members, can be judged in terms of how they confront minorities, outsiders, unfamiliar groups. The ability to accept and appreciate what is different, even alien, marks the mature society and the fully developed individual. It might be called the rule of non-alikes: you may judge and be judged by how non-alikes are confronted. No man is a stranger except to the man trying to live as an island. Carried to an extreme, the totally isolated psyche belongs to the insane man, the totally involved psyche to the saint. The former are the creatures and mouthpieces of despair, the latter of hope.

In our own time, the message of hope has been preached by men of all faiths and of various political commitments. However, Western man too readily restricts his awareness of such philosophies to Western Christianity and Western society, overlooking the insight of historian F. S. C. Northrop that "it should eventually be possible to achieve a society for mankind generally in which the higher standard of living of the most scientifically advanced and theoretically guided Western nations is combined with the compassion, the universal sensitivity to the beautiful, and the abiding equanimity and calm joy of the spirit which characterizes the sages and many of the humblest people of the Orient." [1]

This human harmony, this meeting of East and West, as Northrop calls it, is personified in the public and personal philosophies of charismatic figures all over the world. It is emerging in the enlightened nationalism of many newly developed countries. It is deeply imbedded in the great non-Western religions of Hinduism, Buddhism and Islam, each of them interwoven in the life of Asia and Africa. The color revolution is making it possible for the world family to benefit from the philosophies of hope found in the Afro-Asian parts of the world.

The oldest of the world's organized religions, Hinduism is characterized by tolerance of all beliefs in its course through prehistory and recorded history. Its very beliefs are universalistic in nature, based on one Universal Spirit, without beginning or end, a World Soul, personified in Brahma the creator, Vishnu the preserver, and Shiva the destroyer. Its 300 million adherents (mainly in India, but also in Ceylon, Bali and Thailand) believe, for the most part, in reincarnation that is "earned" by the sum of a person's acts. A Hindu's autobiography leads to his reincarnation; it is a religious view that places responsibility upon the individual.

The caste system that has developed under Hinduism has produced a characteristic often overlooked in the West: the ability to accept and absorb new elements. As Duke University Professor Robert I. Crane notes, "This is done by assigning them and their distinctive traits to a position in the caste system as a new and separate unit. It could be said there is room for everyone in the Hindu household, but each group has its own separate quarters. The unusual tolerance of Hinduism is shown by the willingness of any one caste to let the other castes govern their members by their own distinctive sets of customs and rules." [2] As much as the West rejects the notion of caste as antipathetic to egalitarianism, it is also important to understand the context within which it exists, for Hinduism does offer us a spirit of toleration that is important to the revolution of color.

Such are the ancient roots of organized religion in Asia, that Hinduism gave birth to Buddhism 500 years before the appearance of the Messiah whose life bears many parallels to that of the young Hindu prince who became the Buddha, "The Enlightened." Today, more than 300 million Buddhists in China, Japan, Burma, Mongolia and Southeast Asia adhere to a religion characterized by gentleness, serenity and compassion. Wherever it has a hold—with many local variations—Buddhism, by its commitment to a paramount place in society, elevates spiritual values. In Thailand, for instance, every young man is "drafted"—not into the army but into a monastery, where his head is shaved and he lives for six months as a monk. Throughout their lives, many Buddhists return to the monastery for spiritual refreshment, a habit exemplified by former Premier U Nu of Burma.

In keeping with a religion steeped in legends surrounding the Buddha, who spent 45 years walking from village to village in India imparting his vision, it is appropriate to cite his answer to a question about the ability of different castes to attain salvation. Said Buddha: "I do not admit any difference whatsoever in regard to the nature of their salvation. Just as if, Sire, a man were to kindle a fire with dry herbs, and another man were to kindle a fire with dry salwood, and a third were to kindle a fire with dry mango wood, and a fourth with dry fig

wood—what think you, Sire? Would these diverse fires kindled
with diverse woods show any difference whatsoever in respect
of their flame, hue or brightness?"

This epitomizes the Buddhist teaching on the dignity and
equality of men and its rejection of superiority by virtue of
birth or race. Spiritual and moral achievement is the crucial
criterion of differentiation and it is equally open to all men.
As noted in the authoritative monograph on Buddhism and
race prepared for UNESCO, Buddhists have always stressed
their compatibility with non-Buddhists:

> It is also noteworthy that there were no crusades in Buddhism,
> which never lent itself to imperial expansion and the subjugation
> of peoples. There has been no military or political campaign or
> conquest with the idea of spreading Buddhist culture and civili-
> zation.
> The pacifism of Buddhism, as well as the absence of an "out-
> group" feeling directed towards non-Buddhists on embracing Bud-
> dhism, is perhaps largely responsible for this, as is also the fact that
> the Dhamma (i.e. teachings of the Buddha) is not considered a
> unique revelation which alone contains the sole truth. The Bud-
> dhist definition of the "right philosophy of life" was comprehensive
> enough to contain, recognize and respect whatever truth other reli-
> gions may have.[3]

Islam, sometimes described as a "color-blind" religion, has
in recent years gained many converts in black Africa, adding
to its 400 million adherents in the Middle East, North Africa,
India, Pakistan, Indonesia, Asiatic Russia and China. A comparative latecomer among the major religions, Islam entered
the twentieth century without any history of persecution along
racial lines, having fought its holy wars for religious reasons.

The fierce individualism of Moslems is combined with sim-
plicity of dogma, opening the way to conversion of Asians and
Africans. Professor Morroe Berger of Princeton has even spec-
ulated that "Islam's strong but simple monotheism, its clear
prescriptions for daily life uncomplicated by speculation and

doubt, and its straightforward promises for a pleasurable after-life in reward for piety on earth have so great an appeal in Africa and Asia that it now looks as though Islam, and not Christianity, will be the monotheistic faith of those areas." [4] Indeed, the appeal of Islam to the nonwhite is dramatized by the emergence of the Black Muslims in the United States, reflecting both a need for identity and the appeal of its color blindness.

Against the background of these major Asian and African religions, charismatic figures have arisen in contemporary times as spokesmen for philosophies of hope. None more so than Mahatma Gandhi. Ironically, his method of nonviolent noncooperation was developed in South Africa, where he fought for the civil rights of emigrant Hindus. Led by his dramatic civil-disobedience campaigns, the Hindu masses of India rallied to the cause of India's freedom from British rule.

Said Gandhi, speaking with the accent of the East: "The movement of nonviolent noncooperation has nothing in common with the historical struggles for freedom in the West. It is not based on brute force or hatred. It does not aim at destroying the tyrant. It is a movement of self-purification. It therefore seeks to convert the tyrant."

His wish that it "may be through the Negroes that the unadulterated message of nonviolence will be delivered to the world" found fruition in Martin Luther King. When Dr. King received the Nobel Peace Prize in 1964, he reminded the world of his Gandhian commitment:

The nonviolent resisters can summarize their message in the following simple terms: We will take direct action against injustice despite the failure of governmental and other official agencies to act first. We will not obey unjust laws or submit to unjust practices. We will do this peacefully, openly, cheerfully, because our aim is to persuade. We adopt the means of nonviolence because our end is a community at peace with itself. We will try to persuade with our words, but if our words fail, we will try to persuade with our acts. We will always be willing to talk and seek fair compromise, but we are ready to suffer when necessary and even risk our lives to become witnesses to truth as we see it.

In a courageous warning in London's St. Paul's Cathedral, Dr. King also cautioned that "the doctrine of black supremacy is as great a danger as the doctrine of white supremacy." The first non-Anglican to deliver an Evensong sermon in St. Paul's, Dr. King said of the civil rights struggle: "All over the world as we struggle for justice and freedom, we must never use second-class methods to gain them."

After his sermon, the congregation rose and sang a hymn that began with the following lines, filling the occasion with symbolic hope:

> Once to every man and nation
> Comes the moment to decide,
> In the strife of truth with falsehood,
> For the good or evil side.

And the echo comes from Africa as well as Asia. President Kenneth David Kaunda of Zambia has said: "One of the long-term consequences of racial equality will be the growth of nonracism, i.e., the establishment of a unity beneath racial differences." President Léopold Sédar Senghor of Senegal has said: "We are now all of us, of different features, color, languages, customs, stirred and carried by the same movement of life. We are on our way toward the world of tomorrow, the world of the civilization of the universal." And when that noble African, Albert John Luthuli, a Zulu chief, received the Nobel Prize in 1961, he delivered a memorable manifesto:

In a strife-torn world, tottering on the brink of world destruction by man-made nuclear weapons, a free and independent Africa is in the making, in answer to the injunction and challenge of history: "Arise and shine for thy light is come." Acting in concert with other nations, she is man's last hope for a mediator between

East and West, and is qualified to demand of the great powers to "turn the swords into ploughshares" because two-thirds of mankind is hungry and illiterate; to engage human energy, human skill and human talent in the service of peace, for the alternative is unthinkable—war, destruction and desolation; and to build a world community which will stand as a lasting monument to the millions of men and women, to such devoted and distinguished world citizens and fighters for peace as the late Dag Hammarsjkold, who have given their lives that we may live in happiness and peace.

Speaking from his pinnacle as Secretary-General of the United Nations and, also, from his position as a voice of Asia, His Excellency U Thant has summarized the divisions and the discrimination that threaten mankind and keep the world in a state of precarious tension. In an address on February 20, 1965, that was the climax of an international convocation based on the papal encyclical, "Pacem in Terris," he said in two crucial passages:

Thus, although we have abjured war as an instrument of policy, all nations have not yet abjured the state of mind that has so often led to war—the nationalistic urge to dominate and extend, by various means, their spheres of influence, and the conviction of the unquestionable superiority of their own particular traditions, forms and ways of life. Nor has it been possible effectively to eliminate the use of force, whether openly or covertly, as a means of furthering political or other ends. Such attitudes inevitably breed in other nations the fears, resentments and suspicions which historically have also created the atmosphere of tension in which wars break out. Again, although we speak loudly for equal rights and against discrimination, there are still many nations and groups throughout the world who are not prepared to accept the practical consequences of these ideals, while an even greater number still suffer from discrimination or lack of equal opportunity. It is this failure of everyday, practical behaviour to keep pace with professed ideals and aims which makes the promise of our infinitely promising world a mockery for so many of its inhabitants. . . .
Beneath the present political realignments, the world *is* in fact divided in a number of ways. It is divided economically; it is divided racially; and it is divided ideologically, although this latter division

may prove to be less basic than the first two. These divisions must be faced and discussed with reason and determination. We ignore them at our peril, for if they are allowed to persist and grow larger they will unleash, as they already show signs of doing, darker forces of bigotry, fear, resentment and racial hatred than the world has ever seen. We cannot agree to live in such a nightmare, still less to bequeath it to our children.

Then the Secretary-General ended his address by focusing on the revolution that must take place within the hearts of all men, and the challenge that must be taken up by their leaders:

Governments, however well and sincerely they may cooperate in the United Nations, cannot by themselves face the great and shifting problems of our age in isolation. The peoples they represent must also give life and reality to the aims and ideals of the Charter, towards which we strive. Here again, we now have the means to achieve a great objective, an enlightened world public opinion. One of the revolutions of our age, the revolution in communications of all kinds, has made a well-informed world public opinion technically possible for the first time in history. Our problem is to ensure a beneficial use of these means of communication. This is a challenge to leaders both temporal and spiritual, to intelligent and creative men and women everywhere. Without real knowledge and understanding and without a determination to learn from the past, to rid ourselves of outmoded prejudices and attitudes, and to face the future together with both hope and wisdom, we shall not succeed in making our aims and ideals a working reality. The encyclical *Pacem in Terris* gives us an inspiring lead towards that change of heart which our great aims so urgently require.

From the American South, the voice of white reason is growing louder too, as was evident in the special September 1963 issue of *Ebony* magazine which was devoted to the 100th anniversary of the Emancipation Proclamation. Ralph McGill, editor and publisher of the Georgia newspaper, *Atlanta Constitution,* pointed out: "A free South will be, in fact, a New South. The human condition always has had at least three yearnings . . . to be treated as a human being, to have an equal, fair chance to win respect and advancement as an individual in the economic environment and freely to seek spiritual and cultural happiness." A courageous woman whose family settled in Virginia before the American Revolution, Sarah Patton Boyle, wrote in the same issue of *Ebony* of her own fight against racism in the South and concluded: "I have learned a truth worth every loss: we are not at the mercy of others. Each can choose for himself whether he will be disintegrated by resentment and self-pity or integrated by his own love, by his own will to serve the best in all his fellow men."

Probably the most persuasive and universalistic philosophy of hope to emerge in contemporary times has been set forth by a French Jesuit paleontologist, Pierre Teilhard de Chardin. This visionary depicted a grand scheme for "The Future of Man," a magnificent and optimistic view of evolution toward a unity of mankind. It is a world view that excites many followers and influentials who see in his works a fulfillment of the task he set before himself early in his career: "My sole ambition is to leave behind me the mark of a logical life, directed wholly toward the grand hopes of the world." Such was his impact that he is being called the greatest thinker-prophet of the twentieth century.

His world view is embodied in *The Phenomenon of Man*, published a few months after his death on Easter Sunday in 1955. In it he refers to man as "the ascending arrow of the great biological synthesis." To him, the scheme of evolution is moving mankind toward a "final maturing and ecstasy" that will be a synthesis in spiritual terms—the kind of synthesis that unites all philosophers of hope.

In conceiving of a "noosphere," the sum total of the life of thought, Teilhard projects the convergence toward which mankind is evolving. Omega, as he calls that outcome, is an achievement of the "upflow" of life, a cosmic climax that embraces differences and distinctions in a ceaseless movement toward human solidarity.

The breathtaking twentieth century acceleration of mankind testifies to the optimism of Teilhard: 300 million years ago life appeared on this planet; 100,000 years ago the first man; 30,000 years ago, the first homo sapiens; 10,000 years ago, the first social man. And only 22 years ago, the scientific revolution that offers unlimited devastation as well as unlimited hope. For Teilhard, drawing on his vast knowledge of science, mankind is moving toward a harmonious unity and "we could more easily prevent the earth from turning than Mankind from progressing."

From Teilhard to a Virginia lady who bravely fights for integration, from a Buddhist in Thailand to a Zulu chief, the spirit of reconciliation and of human harmony demonstrates its strength in this most perilous of all centuries. Man has seen the tragedies of the philosophies of separation and alienation and how they lead to hate. The revolution of color has released for all mankind the values of the Afro-Asian peoples. Now their spirit of harmony offers additional inspiration to mankind to look toward the twenty-first century.

It can be summed up in various ways. It is embodied in the necessary legalisms of the Universal Declaration of Human Rights which the United Nations General Assembly unanimously adopted on December 10, 1948: "All human beings are born free and equal in dignity and rights. They are endowed with reason and conscience and should act towards one another in a spirit of brotherhood." Or as Gandhi stated it: "The more efficient a force is, the more silent and the more subtle it is. Love is the subtlest force in the world. . . ."

CHAPTER ELEVEN

AN AMERICAN
OPPORTUNITY

In the conclusion to *An American Dilemma,* his monumental study of the Negro in American life, Gunnar Myrdal described the Negro problem as "not only America's greatest failure but also America's incomparably great opportunity for the future." The dilemma was self-evident; it was the gap between reality and the ideals of the American Creed. A nation created out of a commitment to life, liberty and the pursuit of happiness, a country with inalienable rights, a favored land dedicated to human dignity, violated its basic premises at the expense of Negro Americans.

But the dilemma has become an opportunity that is being faced by the accelerated drive to match ideals and realities. And the world watches as the United States struggles to demonstrate that white and black can live together as equals and partners. As Myrdal remarks, "This is what the world needs to believe. Mankind is sick of fear and of disbelief, of pessimism and cynicism. It needs the youthful, moralistic optimism of America."

The idealism has deep roots in the origins of the United States. It is imbedded in the Declaration of Independence, the Preamble of the Constitution, and particularly Article One of the Bill of Rights—"Congress shall make no law respecting an establishment of religion, or prohibiting the free exercise thereof; or abridging the freedom of speech or of the press; or the right of the people peaceably to assemble and to petition the Government for a redress of grievances."

The spirit of equality, freedom and human dignity has imbued individual Americans—both white and nonwhite—as well as the American spirit, from Patrick Henry to Ralph Bunche. In 1772, Patrick Henry was painfully aware of the shame of slavery and the fact that he had slaves and was "drawn along by the general inconvenience of living here without them." He expressed his mea culpa in a letter: "I will not, I cannot, justify it. However culpable my conduct, I will so far pay my devoir to virtue as to own the excellence and rectitude of her precepts and lament my want of conformity to them." In Ralph Bunche, the American Negro who plays a prominent role in the United Nations Secretariat, the echo is heard in our times and expressed in the accents of equality, an ideal shared even by Americans victimized by prejudice. Mr. Bunche has observed that "every man in the street, white, black, red or yellow knows that this is 'the land of the free.' "

In recent years, this attitude was dramatized by the viewpoints of a prominent Negro public servant and by a former college coed who integrated the University of Georgia. They each insisted on the right to be treated as individual Americans, rather than as Negroes. They demanded what the American Creed offers and testified to the acceptance of that Creed by nonwhite Americans.

Robert C. Weaver, administrator of the U. S. Housing and Home Finance Agency, rejected the special category of Negro-

American in ringing words delivered at a symposium in Chicago:

> My responsibilities as a Negro and an American are part of the heritage I received from my parents—a heritage that included a wealth of moral and social values that do not have anything to do with my race. My responsibilities as a government administrator do not have too much to do with my race, either. My greatest difficulty in public life is combating the idea that somehow my responsibilities as a Negro conflict with my responsibilities as a government administrator: and this is a problem which is presented by those Negroes who feel that I represent them exclusively, as well as by those whites who doubt my capacity to represent all elements in the population. The fact is that my responsibilities as a Negro and a government administrator do not conflict: they complement each other.

After Miss Charlayne Hunter married a white classmate from the University of Georgia, she was confronted by concern about what her interracial marriage would do to the Negro cause. Some liberals wondered whether this would have a negative effect on the Negro civil rights struggle and Charlayne found friends analyzing the effects of the marriage, instead of wishing her happiness. Her answer before network television cameras was a dramatic statement of individuality that is thoroughly American. The reporters addressed their questions to a Negro and were answered by an American: "This [marriage] is a personal thing and my personal life should not have anything to do with that which affects the masses of people. And so I can't be too terribly concerned about that because I have my own life to live."

With the postwar emergence of independent African nations, many American Negroes have looked toward Africa for the source of their cultural identification. Some have even migrated to the African continent hoping to find a better life, only to be disappointed. In an interview with the notable writer on racial matters, Harold Isaacs, one such American said: "I came to Africa feeling like a brother, but there I was, I was not a brother. I was not Senegalese or Nigerian or Ghanian, I was American, an American Negro from an Anglo-Saxon culture, or as much of it as filtered down to me, determining what I am, what I think, what I feel."

Admittedly, the American Negro has an African heritage, but the American Negro and the African Negro have each traveled long distances—often in different directions. There can never be cultural unity, for the differences are too great. Furthermore, the American Negro's so-called loss of identity is not so much loss of his African heritage as the result of the oppression that imposed second-class status upon him.

Finally, the fact of color encourages unity more than cultural similarities and, indeed, the rapport runs deeper than color. It is the rapport of the oppressed that joins nonwhites in America and Africa.

The American Negro is primarily an American. This obvious redundancy needs repeating, particularly in the face of Negro extremists who preach separatism. The overwhelming majority of American Negroes reject this version of segregation just as they reject the Southern version.

A nationwide poll by public-opinion analyst Louis T. Harris in the summer of 1963 bore out the point. The findings, published in *Newsweek,* indicate one consuming goal: integration. Sixty-six percent of all Negroes would live in mixed neighborhoods with whites, if they had the chance. Among lower-income Negroes, who suffer the most from segregation, the figure was even higher—75 percent. Seventy-five percent would prefer to work alongside whites; the figure rises to 88 percent among middle- and upper-income Negroes in the North. Seventy-one percent want their children to attend integrated schools.

The Negroes also share the American dream of a better life

for themselves and their children. Pollster Harris confirmed what Mr. Bunche had observed: a belief in American standards of equality. Negroes chose America 4 to 1 over any other country as the place where minorities, Negroes included, get the fairest chance.

When *Ebony* magazine marked the 100th anniversary of the Emancipation Proclamation with a special issue, the late President John F. Kennedy underlined the accelerated American response to its dilemma:

> The year 1863, when Abraham Lincoln struck off the bonds of slavery, marked the first stage in the emancipation of the American Negro. I believe that future historians, looking back on the brave events of recent months, will regard the year 1963 as the beginning of the final stage—as the great turning-point, when the nation at last undertook to carry the process of emancipation through to its fulfillment. After a century of evasion and delay, the promise of the Emancipation Proclamation is at last on the verge of realization.

For American Negroes, an era of de facto subjugation and gradual emergence reached a turning point in the 1960s. While the process of emancipation was painfully slow and scarred by the misguided philosophy of white supremacists, it had historic American sources. That is a fact often neglected in evaluating the role of America in relation to the universal-pluralistic society. The struggle for Negro equality moved from the moral to the political stage because moral force had, however slowly, been building up.

Because the United States has such a large minority who descended from slavery, the opportunity is as great as is the difficulty of achieving full equality. An added complication is the postwar pressure upon the American economy caused by automation and the emphasis on skill and training. For Negroes, long deprived of advancement through adequate education, the challenge of the economy is an additional handicap. The unskilled whites who feel similar pressures create a hostile atmosphere, as do middle-class whites who hesitate to accept the Negro socially. But this so-called white backlash can only impede, but certainly not turn aside the movement toward full equality.

The Negro looks to the lesson of the American melting pot into which large numbers of newcomers were poured in the nineteenth and early twentieth centuries. While the melting pot was never as complete or as successful as its enthusiasts maintained, it was based on the fundamental American premise of equality and its corollary, equal opportunity. A man was judged for his abilities and for his performance, regardless of race or religion—unless he were a Negro. Now it has finally become the Negro's turn.

In *The Uprooted,* Harvard historian Oscar Handlin has pointed out the capacity for change and improvement that was demonstrated by the immigrant experience and enlarged by it. Professor Handlin comments: "We will not have our nest become again a moldy prison holding us in its tangled web of comfortable habits."

That capacity for change is finally evident in the attitudes of whites favoring civil rights. Estimates on the amount of change and opinions on whether it is large enough vary, but change is there. Possibly the most revealing evidence of the national trend was found by the National Opinion Research Center in a series of national surveys made in 1942, 1956 and 1963. For the first time, in 1963, a majority of all white Americans favored school integration. The trend included the reluctant South. While the percentage of Southerners accepting school integration rose only from 2 to 14 percent between 1942 and 1956, the percentage rose to 34 percent in 1963. Also in 1963, for the first time, Southerners favoring separate Negro sections in cars and buses were in the minority.

Other dramatic changes were found in the South. In 1942,

only 1 out of every 5 Southerners thought Negroes could learn as readily as whites; by 1963, 2 out of 3 Southerners thought so. While only 12 percent of Southerners in 1942 were willing to live near Negroes, by 1963, 44 percent were willing.

In the North, as expected, favorable attitudes were considerably stronger. In 1963, 5 out of 6 Northerners felt that Negroes "can learn things just as well as white people if they are given the same education and training." Two out of 3 Northerners had no objection to residential integration. Among Northern whites living in segregated school districts, 66 percent favored school integration; in Northern areas where the schools were already integrated, 79 percent of the whites favored the policy.

The conclusion of Professor Herbert Hyman of Columbia University summarized the findings: "It is abundantly clear that the attitudes of white Americans, both North and South, are continuing to shift toward greater acceptance of racial integration and that the trend has even accelerated in more recent years."

In a *Newsweek* poll, a companion survey to the Negro survey, Louis Harris also reported in the fall of 1963 that the attitudes of the white South were changing. *Newsweek* said that its poll indicated "that the South is more willing to meet some of its obligations on civil rights than its Congressional delegations realize." Six out of 10 Southerners—8 out of 10 nationally—favored laws to guarantee equal job opportunities.

Overall, the *Newsweek* poll found white America willing to admit its guilt. Nationally, 76 percent of the whites recognize that the Negro is a victim of prejudice, and even in the South this figure was 60 percent. These findings are reminiscent of James Bryce's remark in his book, *The American Commonwealth,* that Americans are willing to face their own shortcomings: "They know, and are content that all the world should know, the worst as well as the best of themselves."

The *Newsweek* polls also produced a revealing comparison of white and Negro attitudes on civil rights issues. There was close agreement among both whites and Negroes on the realities of discrimination: Negro jobs are not equal to those of whites, and Negro education is inferior to that of whites. There was also mutual acceptance of integration in jobs, education and public accommodations. The same percentage of Negroes and whites—77 percent—feel that the Negro job situation will be better in five years. Such optimism, which is so American, undoubtedly stems from the American commitment to the ideal of equality.

However, the poll also underlined the lingering gap between American Negroes and whites. While only 3 percent of the Negroes felt they were moving too fast, 74 percent of the whites thought so. While only 34 percent of the whites thought the Negro revolt was supported by the rank and file, 91 percent of the Negroes thought so. While 42 percent of the whites regarded integrated housing as desirable, 78 percent of the Negroes regarded it as desirable.

Newsweek's poll illustrated a major factor in prejudice—distance. Distance strengthens prejudice. Whites who had social, school and job contacts with Negroes were consistently and significantly less prejudiced in their attitudes. For instance, 48 percent of the whites who never had social contacts with Negroes would object if their child brought a Negro home for supper, while only 17 percent of those who have known Negroes socially would object. In every aspect of the negative traits ascribed to the stereotyped Negro, whites who had social contacts with Negroes were markedly less prejudiced.

Whether the main reason whites had social contacts with Negroes was lack of prejudice or whether prejudice was lessened by such contacts, the reality is that familiarity breeds tolerance. It is happening in America as in the rest of the world.

Despite nasty headlines and vicious incidents, America is moving ahead in its Negro dilemma. It is seizing the opportunity to establish a showcase for the pluralistic society. Just as President Kennedy said, the promise of the Emancipation Proclamation is becoming a reality.

A variety of interlocking factors are pushing America in the right direction. The ideal of the acceptance of man as man has been quickly approached in the area of religious differences. While full ecumenical harmony has not yet been achieved, the hate and fears of one religious group for another have largely disappeared from the American scene. The acceptance and cooperation that exists between the three major faiths has been attained after decades of persistent effort by the leaders involved. This has resulted in the creation of a broad new force —the Protestant-Catholic-Jewish active presence in the social order.

The rapid development of cooperation between the leaders of the churches on major problems has been most recently evident in civil rights. Many observers believe that the full commitment of America's religious leadership assured the passage of the Civil Rights legislation in 1964.

The influence of the religious establishment has been equalled by the impact of the technological era on American economic life. The complexity of modern industrial life has placed great stress on the importance of knowledge, skills and abilities. The competitive-technical demands of a highly diversified society require the best in competence rather than inefficient selection on social nontechnical considerations. This change is just beginning to affect the Negro.

Another factor contributing to the rapid development of a truly pluralistic society is the impact of mass education. With it becoming a matter of almost standard routine that all able young men and women should have at least twelve years of schooling, significant cultural and educational differences between ethnic, religious and racial groups are disappearing. The unprecedented expansion of higher education in the United States and the increasing opportunities for all qualified to obtain a university education are creating a new class that transcends religious, ethnic and racial differences.

Modern transportation and communication have added a dimension of fluidity to American life. Extensive travel within the country and abroad and easy relocation of residence have resulted in the reduction of minority group identifications. This has been especially true among younger generations and university graduates since 1945.

As already noted, substantial support for change is coming from a powerful combination of influential Americans, motivated by religious, political, scientific and humanistic reasons. Stubborn resistance is found among a less powerful and diminishing group motivated by bigotry and hate. Unfortunately, some elements in the lower-income and middle-class groups are still infected with the poison of bigotry. The main driving force among the lower-income and middle-class segments is not hate but fear. Some fear for their jobs and for their "bread and butter," others are concerned with social status. This is especially true of the working classes who regard the rising Negro as a job threat.

Thus far, the lower-income and middle-class groups, which have a high rate of church membership, have not been sufficiently influenced by religious teachings on equality and by the exhortations of those church leaders now overwhelmingly committed to Negro equality. Unless the lower-income and middle-class groups are awakened to the moral challenge and practical necessity of accepting the Revolution of Color, the

United States will lose an historic opportunity to become a showcase for the universal-pluralistic society. The loss would not only be America's, but the world's.

In the past several decades, leadership has been provided by the new religious-scientific-humanistic forces in the United States. This leadership, together with the impact of modern transportation and communications that eliminate all boundaries, has been able to expand the opportunities present in the American system. Now, this leadership is involved in its greatest challenge: extension of the American dream to the Negro people. The success of recent years gives us every reason for optimism. There is an unprecedented opportunity for America to become the showcase for racial harmony. Man needs this inspiration as he moves into the twenty-first century, where technological advances will bring black and white, brown and yellow, into daily contact with each other. Whites and blacks will no longer be separated. What an opportunity for America, with significant numbers of all races within its boundaries, to demonstrate that universal-pluralism is the hope of mankind!

CHAPTER TWELVE

AN OPEN MIND IN ASIA
AND AFRICA

The revolution of color is a revolution in search of a political ideology or, more accurately, a revolution that refuses to uncritically accept outside political ideologies. It is a revolution standing between capitalism and communism, not against them but outside them, despite the brooding presence of the East-West struggle in Asia and Africa.

The revolution has its philosophy of hope and human harmony, its commitment to economic development, its zeal for political independence and, most of all, its faith in the future. The revolution will not accept a political blueprint made in Russia or the United States, nor will the revolution dress itself in American or Soviet clothes. If an ideology emerges, it will be identified only in retrospect after an evolutionary process.

On the one hand, Western capitalism is incompatible with the psychological climate of Africa, Asia and the Caribbean, and beyond the reach of their natural, technological and manpower resources. Capitalism as an economic doctrine is too

123

cold and competitive, too far removed from the spiritually oriented way of life prevalent in these areas. Furthermore, the highly modified form of the capitalist-welfare state in the United States and Europe is viewed as viable only in highly developed nations with a large industrial base. One often hears visitors from the new nations say at the end of a visit to the United States: "Your country is beautiful, the good life, in fact a life of near luxury, but it is possible only in the United States, not in our part of the world."

As already pointed out, the value system of communism has little chance of flowering in the free soil of Africa and Asia, for it is intrinsically alien to the value systems of the people of color. The Communist victory on the Chinese mainland, the only major victory of its kind among the colored races, was the result of a massive series of blunders and historical accidents. Although the Chinese are now conducting a worldwide campaign to convert the other people of color to communism, particularly the Chinese brand, the success of the campaign is limited. The effect has been disruptive rather than constructive—in keeping with Premier Chou En-lai's thesis that "the prospects for revolution are excellent all over Africa." But the Chinese have made few inroads with their claim that they overcame colonialism and are converting their largely peasant economy into a modern industrial state. Their so-called results are seen more and more as a façade of glittering Chinese paper propaganda concealing a country that has been brutalized by communism. On an ideological level, the Chinese have also failed in attempting to establish psychological compatibility between communism and the spiritually oriented way of life common to the colored races.

The new nations stand aloof from both capitalism and communism for another reason. They are determined to avoid any involvement in the ideological struggle of the cold war. Involvement in the cold war amounts to contamination to most leaders of the new nations because it saps meager resources that should be devoted to their all-important war on poverty, illiteracy and disease. The West must realize that the commitment of the new Afro-Asian states to transform their marginal existence is similar to the determination of the Allied Powers to win World War II. The all-out effort is both pervasive and obsessive.

Meanwhile, a parallel phenomenon has taken place in the West. Sociologist Daniel Bell has called it "The End of Ideology." Political panaceas and total blueprints to create Utopian societies are in disrepute. Their simplified and comprehensive views of life, accompanied by a call to action, have become bankrupt in the West. Yet, ironically, the West, and particularly the United States, has not fully confronted this development in approaching the new nations. Too many American leaders and much of American opinion is concerned with exporting what no longer exists in a pure state at home—free-enterprise capitalism. Too many still equate capitalism with democracy, despite the evidence of England, Scandinavia, and Israel.

In arguing that ideology, as a road to action, has reached a dead end, Professor Bell writes:

The two decades between 1930 and 1950 have an intensity peculiar in written history: world-wide economic depression and sharp class struggles; the rise of facism and racial imperialism in a country that had stood at an advanced stage of human culture; the tragic self-immolation of a revolutionary generation that had proclaimed the finer ideals of man; destructive war of a breadth and scale hitherto unknown; the bureaucratized murder of millions in concentration camps and death chambers.

For the radical intellectual who had articulated the revolutionary impulses of the past century and a half, all this has meant an end to chiliastic hopes, to millenarianism, to apocalyptic thinking—and to ideology. For ideology, which once was a road to action, has come to be a dead end.[1]

As many students of the new nations have pointed out, the crucial choice is not between communism and capitalism. Rather, it is a question of what means to pursue in order to develop an underdeveloped nation. The revolution is expressed in rising expectations, but the problem is how to keep faith with the future. The choice is between means to the end; the debate is economic rather than political.

The decision will be made by the emerging influentials and the elite in the new nations since, at the present stage, illiteracy, poverty and disease immobilize their masses. Both the temptations and the prospects present a situation of immense dimensions and many complications.

The temptation is to seek totalitarian means, the temptation dangled in front of the African and Asian nations by the Communists. It is not Communist ideology that poisons, so much as Communist methods—the ruthless, inhuman mobilization of a present generation for the sake of future generations. Today is mortgaged for tomorrow by the Communist method, without regard for the underlying fallacy that the means do not justify the end. Or stated in more pragmatic terms, the means that are destructive defeat the end; a society that brutalizes itself for the future also undermines that future.

While some Asian and African leaders have been demonstrably attracted by this temptation, most leaders of the people of color have shown broadness of vision and breadth of approach. They have an impressive command of radically different cultural contexts: they are at home in village and tribal settings; they move with ease in their diplomatic contacts with the West; they understand Western culture as well as their own; their accent may be Oxford and their tastes cosmopolitan, but their roots are indigenous to Asia and Africa. The West must demonstrate that it can present suitable counterpart officials to communicate with these Asian and African leaders and engage in meaningful dialogue.

In the light of what is happening in Asia and Africa, socialism is taking on great significance, but not as a political ideology. Its significance is as an economic means that is flexible enough to develop local variations. Examples include the socialism of the metaphysical human love of Senghor, the socialism of Teilhard de Chardin's universal society, the highly personal family socialism of Julius Nyerere's "Ujamma." All are either taking root or will take root in the friendly soil of the free nonwhite world. This became so evident to the Vatican that in 1963 the late Pope John XXIII incorporated this reality into his famous encyclical, "Mater et Magistra," pointing out that socialism is a natural approach for the new nations to apply to their fundamental socioeconomic way of life.

This forthright statement was a significant historical development, since many Western thinkers were still carrying on the obsolete nineteenth-century debate between clericalism and freethinking socialism. While some diehards still confuse the issue, Christian thinking in the main recognizes that the humane, spiritually oriented varieties of democratic socialism of Senghor-Chardin-Nyerere are a natural refinement of the value system already prevalent in the new nations.

While socialism will vary according to its national setting, the substance will remain the same: a value system centering on primary consideration for the human individual and emphasizing the obligation of society to assume responsibility for his happiness on earth, while accepting the existence of a Supreme God.

Meanwhile, the mores, important to the masses and imbedded in natural cultures will remain the "way of life" of the new states. For instance, the people of Madagascar will continue to revere their ancestors. In other countries, tribal commitments will remain strong and the traditional dependence of desert nomads on friends will be expressed by placing a high value on personal loyalty.

Even in their approach to democracy, Asian and African leaders will develop their own definitions as they reject doctrinaire versions of what constitutes democracy. For instance, Tom Mboya, who in Kenya typifies the new and enlightened leadership arising among the colored people, argues that democracy does not require the party system as it is known in the West. He says there must be freedom to form parties, but it is not necessary that more than one party should, in fact, exist. His argument, which remains realistic, underlines the groping toward definitions that can fit actual situations:

Perhaps the single-party system will be misused. But has anyone the right or power to stop the sovereign people from decreeing such a system? At the most, we can insist on two things. First, the original decision should be completely voluntary and without any coercion. Secondly, the people should be able, if they so desire, to restore the multi-party system by a further amendment of the constitution . . . My view, therefore, is that the question whether a country is to have a single party or several parties is to be answered not in terms of any preconceived ideas of "democracy" but in the concrete terms of the wishes of the people.[2]

In the evolution and application of their value systems, the colored races will resist any attempt to insert alien values that undermine their fundamental way of life. While various aspects of capitalism and communism may be adapted to their situations as the new nations themselves see fit, any attempt to force fundamental changes will be rejected as a new colonialism. After their own fashion, the people of color will make their own contribution to the emerging civilization that will eventually embrace tomorrow's world.

The resultant ideology will be eclectic, indigenous, variable. It will emerge out of individual situations, free of formalism and of blind ideological commitment. It will be the result of the open mind that characterizes these people in Asia and Africa.

CHAPTER THIRTEEN

THE CHALLENGE AND
THE RESPONSE

In the most profound sense, the revolution of color challenges the fabric of Western society in every aspect of its values and institutions. The challenge and the response are manifest on moral, legal, political and personal levels. The people of color are bringing to judgment the stated beliefs of Western man. They have made it impossible to escape such judgment any longer. Western man is being judged by his actions; verbal postures are no longer enough.

The moral acknowledgment of human dignity and the equality of men is woven inextricably into the cultural and religious commitments of Western man. By turning his back on racial harmony, Western man is rejecting his heritage in the most self-destructive manner possible. Such rejection leaves him an empty shell and his emptiness is proclaimed to the world, an embodiment of moral bankruptcy.

The principle of love among all people is a fundamental cornerstone of Judeo-Christian morality. How unfortunate it is that this cornerstone has been ignored for so long, how unfortunate that racial intolerance is also found in the great non-Christian religions. Although contrary to their teachings, intolerance is practiced by many non-Christians as well as by Christians and Jews.

There are only a few fundamentals in life that are either absolutely right or absolutely wrong and racial tolerance is one of them. As a civilization of men under law, Western society must live by or reject centuries of legal tradition and development. The revolutions of the past—whether French or American—and the turning points of man's compact with authority—whether Magna Charta or Bill of Rights—will be drained of meaning, if racial harmony does not emerge in the world. The people of color no longer seek such legal realities as gifts but demand them as rights.

Most national constitutions in the Western countries postulate equal rights for all, regardless of color, and the legal structures of these nations support constitutional prohibitions against racial discrimination. Modern communications now make it possible for discriminatory acts violating these laws to be given immediate worldwide attention, and make it impossible to camouflage racial discrimination. Western society must either implement the racial equality that it has preached for centuries, or recognize that the colored races will reject dialogue with a Western society that violates its basic orientation by regarding them as inferior.

Political institutions—both on the national and international level—depend on the consent of the governed, and in this time of revolution the nonwhites will only give their consent in return for equality. They will not only refuse to cooperate without such equality; they are reaching the point where they will fight for it.

In Western society, political action in the area of social

change is the special responsibility of its influentials and its leaders. The ordinary man devotes most of his time and attention to the pressing daily requirements of earning a living. But today those who have been given the privilege of leadership in the Western world have a compelling concomitant responsibility to use their political power to make sure that Western society will save itself. Without racial harmony, political chaos within nations and between nations is certain.

The enactment of the United States Civil Rights Act of 1964 is an example of the combined power of moral and political leadership. It was the leadership of the American establishment that brought about the passage of the Civil Rights legislation. The leaders of the three major faiths in the United States played a significant role in clarifying the moral implications to many congressmen who might not have supported the civil rights legislation. The responsible use of the moral-legal-political power of the American establishment in the historic Civil Rights Act of 1964 should set the pattern for future action by leadership groups everywhere in the Western world.

Mankind also depends on the leadership of the people of color. The challenge for them is on one hand the same; on the other, quite different from the challenge facing white leadership. We are all members of the same universal family now living so close to each other. The only alternative to racial harmony is racial fratricide. Nonwhites have so many bitter memories that their leadership, while negotiating and pushing for an end to all indignities, must also inspire their people to forgive the white man for his past sins. The nonwhite leadership is compelled to seek this noble course of action, since prolonged racial hatred will destroy even those who have been the victims of racial oppression.

This opportunity for greatness presented by the revolution of color is accompanied by the threat of destruction. First, increased racial friction would intensify the present uneasy race relationships in the West and result in flaming bitterness. Within the Western world the white man predominates in number, but, particularly in countries like the United States, he is faced with the straightforward demand of the black man for full equal rights. Unless Western whites, especially in the United States and the United Kingdom, accept Negroes as fellow citizen-brothers, increased tension will result. Does any reasonable person want to see street rioting, attacks by police dogs and other acts of uncivilized conduct increase and grow worse?

Of further concern is the danger of alienating the colored people from the Christian Church and from any understanding with the West. The Christian Church must be prepared to accept repudiation by these people if their members persist in their refusal to accord equal human rights. The nonwhites already have serious reservations about the Christian Church as a white man's institution and they will not become second-class members of the white man's church. They will join only as equals.

Further alienation of the colored races would also jeopardize political harmony. The Western nations cannot expect to maintain friendly relations with them when they reject racial equality at home. The only basis for the development of real understanding with the new nations of Africa and Asia is a purge by the white Western nations of superiority-inferiority concepts.

On July 2, 1964, when President Johnson signed the controversial Civil Rights Act, he told the American people that the law's purpose was "not to divide, but to end divisions . . . [and] to promote . . . a more constant pursuit of justice and a deeper respect for human dignity." The President of the United States had signed a comparatively mild legal instrument affirming a revolutionary fact: the emergence of the people of color in his own country and throughout the world.

A little-known bench mark of the revolution in the United States is the fate of an 1875 law, passed in the aftermath of the Civil War. The United States Congress had passed this law guaranteeing Negroes equality in public facilities such as hotels, inns, theaters and conveyances. Eight years later, the U. S. Supreme Court declared the law unconstitutional, holding that the Constitution forbade the states to invade citizens' rights but did not bar such invasion by individuals. Today, such a ruling is inconceivable, reflecting the changing situation facing people of color in the United States and the general consensus among responsible Americans that the Federal Government has a vested interest in the human dignity of all its citizens.

But the dimensions of the color revolution far exceed the legal, the political and the governmental. The social dimensions are both drastic and dramatic and they are imbedded in all the inequities in society and in the tensions that threaten all of its citizens. In the conclusion to his UNESCO monograph on "Racial Myths," Professor Juan Comas summarizes this overriding factor by pointing out the limitations of law and the need to attack underlying conditions:

> More can be done against racial prejudices and myths by endeavouring to amend the conditions which give rise to them.
> Fear is the first of these: fear of war, fear of economic insecurity, fear of loss of personal or group prestige, etc. Racial prejudice in one form or another will continue in the world as long as there is not a greater sense of personal security.[1]

As in the past, the leadership elite must communicate the fact of significant social change to the people at large. In this social revolution, foresight, courage and dedication are needed since the changes overturn centuries-old myths concerning the inferiority of the people of color. Fortunately, Western leadership has grasped the necessity of coming to grips with the revolution of color. The late President Kennedy, an Easterner, and President Johnson, a Southerner, have both epitomized the response to this challenge. In addition, Catholic, Protestant and Jewish leaders have committed their energies, as have civic, welfare and business leaders.

But in all these major areas of Western society—church, state, business and civic life—the initiative of the leadership has not been fully translated into popular acceptance and action. An important reason is the lack of adequate support from the second echelons of leadership. Without such support, the impetus given by leadership cannot reach the public at large.

Meanwhile, the revolution of color is taking place now; by the end of the century it will be complete. If white leadership is unable to inspire the general public to accept the fact of the revolution and its implications, the results will endanger both the white people and mankind as a whole. On the other hand, with general adjustment, mankind can look hopefully toward the year 2000 as the beginning of the era of universal pluralism.

In view of the magnitude of the challenge, the response must be multiple; a composite of the moral, legal, educational and personal. In the moral realm, the Judeo-Christian impact in the white West must be mobilized. Synagogues and Christian churches should launch an unrelenting grass-roots campaign against racial prejudice. Since prejudices run deeply, the effort must be constant and sustained and must be enthusiastically supported by all local clergy. Such an effort, based on the value of charity shared by all branches of Judaism and Christianity, would also provide an opportunity to wage a joint campaign in keeping with the new ecumenical spirit.

The churches must exercise their age-old right and duty to provide moral leadership. Racial prejudice, a transgression against charity, is a major sin against the law of God. The various churches have different ways of censuring their members who flaunt God's laws. They must apply these censures.

The Catholic Church refuses the sacrament of Holy Communion to members who violate her rules concerning abortion. Some Protestant churches will not admit to the Communion rail those who drink alcoholic beverages. These are severe penalties which enable these churches to deter their members from violating church tenets. Certainly, the sin of racism is a major offense against the law of God, as it offends His greatest commandment—Charity. It is difficult to accept the fact that the churches have tolerated, until now, the extreme transgression of racism without invoking extreme sanctions.

While most Western nations have enacted legislation against racial discrimination, it is also necessary that civic, welfare and business organizations add their weight. These groups require their members and employees to refrain from scandalous conduct or from activities injurious to their organizations. This has reduced open religious bias, and such efforts should be intensified.

Society must also adopt a long-range approach. This can be done through a concerted educational program beginning in the elementary school and extending through the university. Broad educational efforts can also be conducted through adult and community education programs.

Ultimately, the problem of color must be solved on an individual basis, with white confronting nonwhite in a spirit of understanding. It is abundantly clear that this will require a revolution in individual psychology to match the political revolution sweeping the world. The revolution of color has microscopic as well as macroscopic dimensions.

Each white person must personally move as quickly as possible to eliminate his superiority-inferiority attitudes toward

nonwhites. Now that blacks and whites are next-door neighbors, prejudices cannot be hidden by remoteness. "Window
dressing" and tokenism will not hide realities, but manifestations of superiority will only cease when attitudes of superiority
have been eliminated.

Even in pluralistic societies like the United States there is
very little close contact and communication between whites
and nonwhites. While legal equality exists in the United States,
with the exception of the South, most white Americans do not
have nonwhites in their intimate circle of friends. Even white
liberals who actively promote Negro causes are notorious for
not having any intimate Negro friends. Their friends in effect
form two circles.

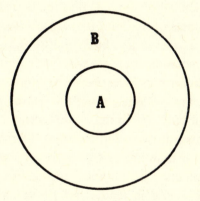

In circle "B," most white liberals have a large number of
acquaintances with whom they maintain social contacts. In
this group are business and academic colleagues, associates
and civic-minded citizens. In this large informal grouping,
many urban liberal whites have some nonwhite acquaintances.
Circle "A" is a small handful of intimate friends. Within this
circle, few liberals active on behalf of Negro causes have
any Negro friends. This is the crux of the problem; even liberals lack close Negro friends.

The wounds of past bitterness are so deep that it is difficult to foresee racial harmony until more intimacy is developed among those leaders who set the tone for human relationships in their community. The visceral antipathy to intermarriage dramatizes this cleavage, for these same liberals argue against any kind of intermarriage between the races. What greater insult could there be to the man of color? Much of the white world is still saying: we may give you equal rights, but we warn you against marrying our daughters!

But my purpose is neither to advocate nor to repudiate intermarriage; it is to underline the abiding cleavage between white and nonwhite. Marriage must remain a matter between the two individuals concerned, free of harsh and irrational pressures from society. It is clear that the door has been closed to intimate contacts of the kind that sustain the society of men in times of sadness and of joy. Such relationships sustain men in their deeply personal encounters with life's uncertainties. Such contacts, which form bridges between cultures and between human groups, are evident among Christians and Jews, Irish and Italians, but only within the white family. Now these same intimate contacts must develop between the races.

If we expect the man in the street to overcome age-old prejudices, these contacts must be encouraged between whites and nonwhites. Here those in leadership positions have a special responsibility. Leadership in all groups—churches, civic bodies, business and welfare groups—must be a public example of "Circle A" friendships between members of different races. Examples of such racial fraternity are already evident. Black and white clergymen are joining forces; whites and nonwhites are forging new friendships in the Peace Corps as they serve side by side in their crusade against poverty, illiteracy and disease. Examples multiply, particularly on the campuses of the United States.

Undoubtedly, intermarriages will increase when there is real communication between people. But they will evolve naturally as marriages between various ethnic and religious groups developed within the white community. Can there be any greater expression of the fatherhood of God over all mankind than the consecration of love between a white and a black before the Divine Altar? It is ironic that interracial marriages seem to be feared even by some religious leaders, who thereby deny the universal Fatherhood of God and the dignity of all men.

When great physical and psychological distances separated racial groups, philosophies of separation—always morally wrong—were not an immediate threat to the well-being of mankind. Today they are exactly that. The hatreds encouraged by segregation and apartheid lead to racial bloodbaths and their effects spread out, infecting the entire world.

In this analysis of the revolution of color, we have reached the final frontier—the willingness of man to meet his fellow man on all levels as his equal. We reach the moment of truth when each man defines his own version of equality, a definition too easily dominated by superficial factors and external pressures. Each man must answer to himself whether he believes in human dignity and human equality; he must decide whether he imposes any limit that denies his stated belief in equality.

Now that the revolutionary social change is underway, the barriers are being broken down in rapid succession, and confrontations arise on more and more intimate levels. The fallen barriers cannot be resurrected nor can the multiplication of contacts be slowed down. Sooner or later, total confrontation will take place on the most intimate levels. The later, the harsher, the harder and the bloodier. The sooner, the easier, the more harmonious and the more beneficial for all mankind. Does man really have a choice?

CHAPTER FOURTEEN

HOPE FOR A NEW CENTURY

In the end, we turn to man. He is the answer, the common denominator, the repository of hope and hate, of pessimism and optimism, the product of the past, the custodian of the present, the maker of the future.

Man can create one world for the sake of Christ or the sake of Krishna or move forward from worldly starting points— whether it is a dialectic of dialogue or a dialogue of dialectic. But let us move, one toward the other, out of a sense of idealism or an acceptance of realities. Or both.

We have no choice.

This lack of a choice, as a last resort, forces man to confront and accept his fellow man. The alternatives to that acceptance of man's oneness are chaos, destruction and annihilation. We must accept the revolution of color, which is nothing less than the intense expression of that wonderful oneness that will not only save us, but move us forward to the next century and the threshold of one world, one civilization.

That single civilization will not ruthlessly erase differences of geography, history, sociology, technology and culture, but it will be a fruitful coalition of differences. That coalition will raise all men—in grey flannel, in saffron robe, in multicolored toga, in fedora, in turban, in shoes, in sandals—to the fullest heights of their potential. By sharing, men receive more than they give.

Nor does mankind lack a starting point. Not all men believe in the City of God, but all believe in the City of Man. A common belief runs through the various value systems of mankind, from the this-worldly views of communism to the other-worldly views of Christianity, from libertarian capitalism at its extreme to repressive communism at its worst. The common belief is that man's problems are surmountable, that he is not doomed to destroy himself and his uneasy world. It is a shared belief that does not depend on blind Utopian commitment, but on the expanding means available to mankind in pursuit of its ends.

The result would be a world with less hunger, less disease and less illiteracy—each lessening in geometric rather than arithmetic proportions. It would be a world in which information, technology and know-how would not be monopolized but shared, a world in which man's common needs and common problems would be the basis for cooperation.

The natural beginning is in racial harmony on a global scale —the concern of this book—the area where a crucial breakthrough can take place. Long-standing problems are not solved overnight, but in any spectrum of problems breakthrough areas stand out. Racial harmony offers such an opportunity, opening the way to expanding solutions in other aspects of man's pursuit of a better life and a world in harmony with itself.

Once reconciliation of the races takes place, man will have accepted man. Then one culture will complement another culture and mankind can move to a new universal pluralism. Here a new harmony between the white West and the new Afro-Asian states would replace the old superior-inferior relationships. This is the opportunity for greatness—to quickly transform the tensions of color into the harmony of mutual acceptance.

Armed with this source of reciprocal strength, the West and the people of color can then seek a basis for a universal pluralism that will accommodate peacefully the believing value systems of the West and the people of color, and the nonbelieving value systems of the Communist consortium.

As man resolves the racial challenge, he can meet with increased optimism the threat of nuclear destruction. It is not farfetched to see in one basic reconciliation the seeds of other reconciliations, the opening toward the hope that man will demonstrate his problem-solving powers in human as well as in technical areas.

The crucial ingredients are the conscience of mankind and the universal dream of a better world. They can provide the motive power to propel the world in the direction of new hope and fundamental progress. Mankind has long waited for the human family to unite and live in harmony and to stress the fundamental similarities between men rather than their accidental differences. No man need surrender his beliefs, only recognize humanity's common grounds for hope. The realization of this civilization of harmony depends a great deal on the efforts of those men who have the power to bring about significant changes. We must, therefore, look to those institutions that not only possess the moral basis for realizing the dignity of man, but whose decisions can bring about substantial change. It is the white man who still possesses this decision-making power; and it is the West that is predisposed philosophically to establishing this community of which we dream.

It is more evident than ever that the two major manifestations of Western leadership must lead the effort to achieve cultural dialogue and racial equality. They are the United States, as political leader of the Western world, and the Judeo-Christian community of churches, as the sources of the West's moral mandate. Fortified with the courage and strength of people who believe, Western man and the man of color can then pursue understanding and dialogue with the men who do not believe. The prospects have become encouraging, for the combined political and religious leadership is aware, concerned and at work.

In the end, we turn to man and to our faith in mankind. In the end, we turn to our belief in man's ability to confront and conquer his challenges. In the end, imbued with a commitment to man's dignity, we are optimistic.

I believe in man!

APPENDICES

Three African leaders have expressed themselves on various aspects of racial harmony. Doctor Léopold Sédar Senghor, the poet-philosopher President of Sénégal, spoke enthusiastically about the people of color and the white people moving together "towards the world of tomorrow, the world of the civilization of the universal," when he visited Fordham University in New York City on November 2, 1961. Albert John Luthuli, 1960 Nobel Peace Prize Winner, offered the hand of reconciliation in his address at Oslo, Norway on December 10, 1961. On the other hand, the late Patrice Lumumba forcefully mirrored the racial scars of white rule in his independence day address in Leopoldville on June 30, 1960. Excerpts from President Senghor's address are included in appendix I and the full addresses of Mr. Luthuli and the late Congo Premier, Mr. Lumumba, are included in appendices II and III.

APPENDIX I

Address by
His Excellency, Léopold Sédar Senghor
President, the Republic of Sénégal
Fordham University

Thursday, November 2, 1961

In my own country, the country of the man who comes to visit you today, to know (connaître) means to be born with, to be born anew (con-naître) and signifies also to die in order to be reborn. I do not bring you anything else except the readiness and the humility of a very ancient people, who have known the vicissitudes of history, but who have never lost faith in themselves and in the future of mankind. This is then the message of our universities of Black Africa, which are a school of life.

To this readiness and humility we have added the method of Europe. This means that we have rejected and that we will

146

continue to reject isolation, even a splendid isolation. We must admit that our relations with Europe have not always been smooth, but these difficulties prove that there has been a contact between two civilizations. It is true also that Europe has destroyed in our countries many values worthy of consideration, but it was in order to bring us other values to replace our own. We have transformed European values into complements of our own values, meaning that we have stamped them with the seal of Black Africa. By so doing we have remained faithful to ourselves and to history, and we have accomplished this without creating among us any complexes. The reality of history is constituted by the presence in the United States of America of 17 million Negroes, who came from Africa with sweat on their brows, rhythm in their hearts, strength in their arms. These Negroes have left their mark in the life of the most powerful nation in modern times. Nowhere else could one be more conscious of this historical reality than here at Fordham, and the best proof is to be found on the shelves of your library which display, side by side, books on the French Revolution and on the American Revolution. A momentous fact occurred in the first ten years of your University, of great importance for the countries of Black Africa. The abolition of slavery in Europe took place seven years after the foundation of St. John's College by Archbishop Hughes. A few years before, the American Society for the Defense of the Black Race had decided to transplant on the African coast, former slaves to whom freedom had been restored. Thus was born the Republic of Liberia, a neighboring country, with whom the Republic of Sénégal maintains relations of friendship and brotherly love, within an association known today as the Monrovia Group.

Historians have underlined the importance of the Act of April 27, 1848. It marked a turning point in the evolution of the world even though it was only the result of a generous impulse of a rather narrow-minded bourgeoisie. The importance of this Act lies essentially in the idea that it created in this return to "normal life." This was certainly not a surprise for the Negroes of America who, for many years, through their Negro blues and spirituals had kept alive what the poet Aimé Césaire has called "the bitter taste for liberty."

The revolutionaries of 1848 were not, indeed, political men. They were poets. This explains their vision of a generous world arising in a spirit of brotherhood. They were the first to dream of a total liberation of man. It is true also that the revolutionary poets of 1848 were the brothers of the tribunes of 1793. I know that at Fordham there is a great French Revolution. The teaching of history is a means of assessing the possibilities of the future while remaining in touch with the past. Above all, it makes it possible to cast on daily events the light of past experiments. Archbishop Hughes had understood that lesson, endowed, as he was, with such a keen vision of the future.

We are then, ladies and gentlemen of Fordham, at a crossroad. In New York, in this city which people carelessly have called heartless, your mission is to maintain an island of hope. Your University, as I have said, enjoys an international reputation. It is above all a place where men of different races, different countries, different philosophies, may meet each other. This was also the vision of Archbishop Hughes—to start from one's own data and to accede to a deeper knowledge of other continents, of other people. Such is the method that Negro-Africans apply in approaching the world. It is a sign and an expression of readiness.

At Fordham, you are the dispensers of science, that is to say, of knowledge. You teach law, which is a method to govern society; education, which is the art to raise children; pharmacy, which is the preservation of health. You teach the arts and sciences, which are manifestations of the genius of man; philosophy, which is the rule of life; finally, the sciences, which are means of investigation and discovery. You have understood your mission which is to arm these young men and women for the struggle which is life. Your vocation consists in training them to be responsible and open-minded men and women.

Turning now to you, students of Fordham University, I cannot resist the temptation to quote these verses, which you know so well, of the poet Walt Whitman, the most powerful poet of America, by his inspiration, his vision and his strength. In the manner of the African patriarchs, Walt Whitman said:

> I announce myriads of youths, beautiful,
>   gigantic, sweet-blooded,
> I announce a race of splendid and savage old men.

Young men and young women of America, you have the good fortune to be able to face a world devoted to the philosophy of the absurd carrying as your viaticum the hope sung by Walt Whitman. For it is, indeed, a matter of hope. Whitman teaches you a way of being, a way of life. Poet, he is solidly rooted in his soil but he gazes upon and embraces the entire world. He was a man in a state of readiness. He was a man faithful in friendship and his eyes were resolutely turned towards the future.

The greatest lyric poet of the United States of America has given us a splendid lesson in humanism, which is expressed in the following verses:

> And what I assume, you shall assume,
> For every atom belongs to me, as good belongs
>   to you.

Such is the message that a poet who is not only a poet of America, but a poet of the world, transmits to you. It expresses a humanistic vision of the world. It announces an ideal.

It is now your duty, drawing upon your youthful enthusiasm, to keep this ideal alive. You are now responsible of a world which has been shaped by your predecessors. You have traditions to be maintained, dreams to be realized, a vision to be extended. If your predecessors were kind men, you must be kind men also, but with a strong will. You have been trained in traditions based on the respect of the human person. In this University, you will learn to be modest and to work, according to tested methods. You will leave Fordham proud possessors of enviable academic titles; but these titles will not help you in resolving all the problems which will be presented to you. Your academic titles will give you the ability to face these problems, but their solution will be dependent upon the way in which you will face them, I mean in your method.

What now will be these problems which will be presented to you, any which will call urgently for an answer? They will be the problems of a man, who, in a world of science and of techniques, is seeking his balance. Armed with the knowledge which is now imparted to you by your eminent masters, you will have to find your true selves, and realize all your potentialities. You will need more than courage, more than perspicacity. You will need to remain in a state of readiness, as we are in the Negro-African tradition. You will have to tame a world in the manner of the first men. Needless to say, oceans and forests will no longer constitute obstacles for you. But you will face harsh realities. You will think that you are in another world when the problem will be to conquer hunger, ignorance, disease, poverty in a world which seems to be so well provided. It will be difficult for you to think that, at a time when automation reigns supreme and when the most varied foods are produced by machines, in other parts of this planet, other men seek their livelihood by the strength of their arms, with the most primitive tools. But you will not be surprised by the hope of these millions of men who know full well that they are backward and yet refuse to yield to pessimism, refuse to be discouraged. You will not be surprised because Walt Whitman will already have told you:

> A worship new I sing,
> You captains, voyagers, explorers, yours,
> Your engineers, you architects, machinists, yours,
> You, not for trade or transportation only,
> But God's name, and for thy sake O soul.

But people of Fordham University, you are being taught, in this very place, that you won't be alone in the world which awaits you. In Black Africa, young people like yourselves, share the same preoccupations, the same concern. These young people also are hungry and thirsty for knowledge. They know full well that they must bring their contribution to build the civilization of the universal, which will be the work of all, or shall not be. Therefore, the will of the young people of Africa is to start from the original foundation of Negro-African civilization, enlightened and enriched by the contributions of Europe and to meet you at the appointed time. The skeptics will say that this is an impossible ambition, but it is a human ambition, at the measure of Africa, at the measure of the world, which will be built tomorrow.

Like yourselves, the young people of Black Africa are in the process of preparing their arms, of forming their minds in the disciplines which now govern the world. They have a keen consciousness of their "situation." Living in a country which is now in the process of being developed, their action has a double meaning: to follow closely the present reality and to look into the future. By so doing, they will have remained faithful to the tradition of their people. Our young people know that it is impossible for them to remain idle, apart from the great movement of history. They know that nature can be tamed, that the means offered by a technical civilization can be of great help to them. The tasks which confront them are, indeed, staggering. But from the education of children to the creation of a great road system, the process is essentially the same. No one will speak henceforth of Promethean projects, but what is being achieved now in the fully developed countries thanks to scientific methods and technical means deserves to retain our attention.

Yet, the real originality of this revolution lies elsewhere. From the spark created by the confrontation of two civilizations, the young people of Africa have drawn a flame which will light their way. This process presupposes not only a necessary return to the original sources, but also an opening on the world outside, particularly on Europe and her daughter, America. Europe is proud to call herself the daughter of reason and, by a dialectical method, she has tackled the problems of her evolution. For a long time, she has imposed her views on the rest of the world. On this last point, she has erred. By that, I mean that the triumph of European reason has been harmful to Europe, because it has prevented Europe from becoming aware that other forms of reason may exist elsewhere. The Negro-African reason is also dialectical since it is based on a communion, on a form of knowledge obtained through sympathy. If the European is a bird of prey, the Negro-African remains earthly, that is to say, all senses. Aimé Césaire had said of him that he is porous to all the inspirations of the world. These two attitudes are not contradictory, but rather complement each other, and from their union, the civilization of tomorrow, the New Man will be born. The contribution of Africa will be to bring into the evolution of the world an element of love, since love is also a confrontation of two attitudes. Having started from our own philosophy, we have approached without apprehension, the philosophy of Europe.

Without apprehension, indeed, yet with real humility. Our own vocation is to demonstrate that, among the European methods of constructing the world there is room for other values, the values in which all people believe. One will not be surprised then to learn that our own experience leads to a constructive critique of European reason.

European reason is abstract mainly because it has willfully forsaken spiritual values. Instead of abstraction we have chosen another principle, a principle of reunion, orientated towards a complete communion of all people. In order to be really constructive, this principle must rely on the spiritual forces of man. Our attitude is then one of conciliation between the external and the internal realities of the world. The African socialist way, which was born on the banks of the Sénégal River, is nothing else but this lucidness and this love before nature, this courage to face the other through sympathy. Such will be the contribution of our continent to the civilization of the universal. Then a new race of men will appear on the earth, a race of pioneers, full of endeavor, "playing the very game of the world." They will be men without prejudices, and men who "will give light wings to reason." It is this new race which Walt Whitman announced in the following verses:

> A world of new primitives has risen with
>   perspectives of incessant and increased life:
> A musty and active race is installing and
>   organizing itself.
> I sing of a new cult, I dedicate it to you
>   —Captain, Navigator, Explorer—
> To you, Engineer, to you, Architect, to you,
>   Machine maker.
> Come to me, I wish to create the indissoluble
>   continent,
> I wish to make the most magnificent race
>   upon which the sun has ever shone,

I wish to make admirable, magnetic countries,
    with brotherly love
Which lasts as long as the life of the comrades,
I wish to plant brotherly love as strong as
    the trees which bear the flowers of
    America and the shores of the great lakes
    and which cover the prairie.
I wish that the cities become inseparable.
Their arms around the neck of one another. . . .

Distinguished professors, students of Fordham University, a poet has shown you the way, the way of hope and of courage. Walt Whitman, the poet of America thus meets Archbishop Hughes, founder of your University, the sages of Africa and of Asia, the masters of sciences of Europe. Man is saved since his hope has been maintained. We are now, all of us, of different features, color, languages, customs, stirred and carried by the same movement of life. We are on our way toward the world of tomorrow, the world of the civilization of the universal.

APPENDIX II

Address of Albert John Luthuli
Zulu African Chief and 1960 Nobel Peace Prize Winner
Delivered at the Nobel Peace Prize Award
Oslo, Norway, December 10, 1961

In years gone by, some of the greatest men of our century have stood here to receive this Award, men whose names and deeds have enriched the pages of human history, men whom future generations will regard as having shaped the world of our time. None could be left unmoved at being plucked from the village of Groutville, a name many of you have never heard before and which does not even feature on many maps—to be plucked from banishment in a rural backwater, to be lifted out of the narrow confines of South Africa's internal politics and placed here in the shadow of these great figures. It is a great honour to me to stand on this rostrum where many of the great men of our times have stood before.

The Nobel Peace Award that has brought me here has for me a threefold significance. On the one hand it is a tribute to my humble contribution to efforts by democrats on both sides of the colour line to find a peaceful solution to the race problem. This contribution is not in any way unique. I did not initiate the struggle to extend the area of human freedom in South Africa; other African patriots—devoted men—did so before me. I also, as a Christian and patriot, could not look on while systematic attempts were made, almost in every department of life, to debase the God-factor in man or to set a limit beyond which the human being in his black form might not strive to serve his Creator to the best of his ability. To remain neutral in a situation where the laws of the land virtually criticised God for having created men of colour was the sort of thing I could not, as a Christian, tolerate.

On the other hand the Award is a democratic declaration of solidarity with those who fight to widen the area of liberty in my part of the world. As such, it is the sort of gesture which gives me and millions who think as I do, tremendous encouragement. There are still people in the world today who regard South Africa's race problem as a simple clash between Black and White. Our government has carefully projected this image of the problem before the eyes of the world.

This has had two effects. It has confused the real issues at stake in the race crisis. It has given some form of force to the government's contention that the race problem is a domestic matter for South Africa. This, in turn, has tended to narrow down the area over which our case could be better understood in the world.

From yet another angle, it is welcome recognition of the role played by the African people during the last fifty years to establish, peacefully, a society in which merit and not race, would fix the position of the individual in the life of the nation.

This Award could not be for me alone, nor for just South Africa, but for Africa as a whole. Africa presently is most deeply torn with strife and most bitterly stricken with racial conflict. How strange then it is that a man of Africa should be here to receive an Award given for service to the cause of peace and brotherhood between men. There has been little peace in Africa in our time. From the northern-most end of our continent, where war has raged for seven years, to the centre and to the south there are battles being fought out, some with arms, some without. In my own country, in the year of 1960 for which this Award is given, there was a state of emergency for many months. At Sharpeville, a small village, in a single afternoon 69 people were shot dead and 180 wounded by small arms fire; and in parts like the Transkei, a state of emergency is still continuing. Ours is a continent in revolution against oppression. And peace and revolution make uneasy bedfellows. There can be no peace until the forces of oppression are overthrown.

Our continent has been carved up by the great powers; alien governments have been forced upon the African people by military conquest and by economic domination; strivings for nationhood and national dignity have been beaten down by force; traditional economics and ancient customs have been disrupted, and human skills and energy have been harnessed for the advantage of our conquerors. In these times there has been no peace; there could be no brotherhood between men.

But now, the revolutionary stirrings of our continent are setting the past aside. Our people everywhere from north to south of the continent are reclaiming their land, their right to participate in government, their dignity as men, their nationhood. Thus, in the turmoil of revolution, the basis for peace and brotherhood in Africa is being restored by the resurrection of national sovereignty and independence, of equality and the dignity of man.

It should not be difficult for you here in Europe to appreciate this. Your continent passed through a longer series of revolutionary upheavals, in which your age of feudal backwardness gave way to the new age of industrialization, true nationhood, democracy and rising living standards—the golden age for which men have striven for generations. Your age of revolution, stretching across all the years from the eighteenth century to our own, encompassed some of the bloodiest civil wars in all history. By comparison, the African revolution has swept across three-quarters of the continent in less than a decade; its final completion is within sight of our own generation. Again, by comparison with Europe, our African revolution—to our credit, is proving to be orderly, quick and comparatively bloodless.

This fact of the relative peacefulness of our African revolution is attested to by other observers of eminence. Professor C. W. de Kiewiet, President of Rochester University, U.S.A., in a Hoernle Memorial Lecture for 1960, has this to say: "There has, it is true, been almost no serious violence in the achievement of political self-rule. In that sense there is no revolution in Africa—only reform. . . ."

Professor D. V. Cowen, then Professor of Comparative Law at the University of Cape Town, South Africa, in a Hoernle Memorial Lecture for 1961, throws light on the nature of our struggle in the following words: "They (the whites in South Africa) are, again fortunate in the very high moral calibre of the nonwhite inhabitants of South Africa, who compare favourably with any on the whole continent." Let this never be forgotten by those who so eagerly point a finger of scorn at Africa.

Perhaps by your standards, our surge to revolutionary reforms is late. If it is so—if we are late in joining the modern age of social enlightenment, late in gaining self-rule, independence and democracy, it is because in the past the pace has not been set by us. Europe set the pattern for the nineteenth and twentieth century development of Africa. Only now is our continent coming into its own and recapturing its own fate from foreign rule.

Though I speak of Africa as a single entity, it is divided in many ways—by race, language, history and custom; by political, economic and ethnic frontiers. But in truth, despite these multiple divisions, Africa has a single common purpose and a single goal—the achievement of its own independence. All Africa, both lands which have won their political victories, but have still to overcome the legacy of economic backwardness, and lands like my own whose political battles have still to be waged to their conclusion—all Africa has this single aim: our goal is a united Africa in which the standards of life and liberty are constantly expanding; in which the ancient legacy of illiteracy and disease is swept aside, in which the dignity of man is rescued from beneath the heels of colonialism which have trampled it. This goal, pursued by millions of our people with revolutionary zeal, by means of books, representations, demonstrations, and in some places armed force provoked by the adamancy of white rule, carries the only real promise of peace in Africa. Whatever means have been used, the efforts have gone to end alien rule and race oppression.

There is a paradox in the fact that Africa qualifies for such an Award in its age of turmoil and revolution. How great is the paradox and how much greater the honour that an Award in support of peace and brotherhood of man should come to one who is a citizen of a country where the brotherhood of man is an illegal doctrine, outlawed, banned, censured, proscribed and prohibited; where to work, talk or campaign for the realization in fact and deed of the brotherhood of man is hazardous, punished with banishment, or confinement without trial, or imprisonment; where effective democratic channels to peaceful settlement of the race problem have never existed these 300 years; and where white minority power rests on the most heavily armed and equipped military machine in Africa. This is South Africa.

Even here, where white rule seems determined not to change its mind for the better, the spirit of Africa's militant struggle for liberty, equality and independence asserts itself. I, together with thousands of my countrymen have in the course of the struggle for these ideals, been harassed, and imprisoned, but we are not deterred in our quest for a new age in which we shall live in peace and in brotherhood.

It is not necessary for me to speak at length about South Africa; its social system, its politics, its economics and its laws have forced themselves on the attention of the world. It is a museum piece in our time, a hangover from the dark past of mankind, a relic of an age which everywhere else is dead or dying. Here the cult of race superiority and of white supremacy is worshipped like a god. Few white people escape corruption and many of their children learn to believe that white men are unquestionably superior, efficient, clever, industrious and capable; that black men are, equally unquestionably, inferior, slothful, stupid, evil and clumsy. On the basis of the mythology that "the lowest amongst them is higher than the highest amongst us," it is claimed that white men build everything that is worth while in the country; its cities, its industries, its mines and its agriculture, and that they alone are thus fitted and entitled as of right to own and control these things, whilst black men are only temporary sojourners in these cities, fitted only for menial labour, and unfit to share political power. The Prime Minister of South Africa, Dr. Verwoerd, then Minister of Bantu Affairs, when explaining his government's policy on African education had this to say: "There is no place for him (the African) in the European community above the level of certain forms of labour."

There is little new in this mythology. Every part of Africa which has been subject to white conquest has, at one time or another, and in one guise or another, suffered from it, even in its virulent form of the slavery that obtained in Africa up to the nineteenth century. The mitigating feature in the gloom of those far-off days was the shaft of light sunk by Christian missions, a shaft of light to which we owe our initial enlightenment. With successive governments of the time doing little or nothing to ameliorate the harrowing suffering of the black man at the hands of slave-drivers, men like Dr. David Livingstone and Dr. John Philip and other illustrious men of God stood for social justice in the face of overwhelming odds. It is worth noting that the names I have referred to are still anathema to some South Africans. Hence the ghost of slavery lingers on to this day in the form of forced labour that goes on in what are called farm prisons. But the tradition of Livingstone and Philip lives on, perpetuated by a few of their line. It is fair to say that even in present day conditions, Christian missions have been in the vanguard of initiating social services provided for us. Our progress in this field has been in spite of, and not mainly because of the government. In this the Church of South Africa —though belatedly, seems to be awakening to a broader mission of the Church, in its ministry among us. It is beginning to take seriously the words of its Founder who said "I came that they might have life and have it more abundantly." This is a call to the Church in South Africa to help in the all-round development of MAN in the present, and not only in the hereafter. In this regard, the people of South Africa, especially those who claim to be Christians, would be well advised to take heed of the Conference decisions of the World Council of Churches held at Cottesloe, Johannesburg, in 1960, which gave a clear lead on the mission of the Church in our day. It left no room for doubt about the relevancy of the Christian message in the present issues that confront mankind. I note with gratitude this broader outlook of the World Council of Churches. It has a great meaning and significance for us in Africa.

There is nothing new in South Africa's apartheid ideas, but South Africa is unique in this: the ideas not only survive in our modern age, but are stubbornly defended, extended and bolstered up by legislation at the time when in the major part of the world they are now largely historical and are either being shamefacedly hidden behind concealing formulations, or are being steadily scrapped. These ideas survive in South Africa because those who sponsor them profit from them. They provide moral whitewash for the conditions which exist in the country: for the fact that the country is ruled exclusively by a white government elected by an exclusively white electorate which is a privileged minority; for the fact that 87 percent of the land and all the best agricultural land within reach of town, market and railways is reserved for white ownership and occupation and now through the recent Group Areas legislation nonwhites are losing more land to white greed; for the fact that all skilled and highly paid jobs are for whites only; for the fact that all universities of any academic merit are an exclusive preserve of whites; for the fact that the education of every white child costs about £64.p.a.; whilst that of an African child costs about £9.p.a. and that of an Indian child or coloured child costs about £20.p.a.; for the fact that white education is universal and compulsory up to the age of sixteen, whilst education for the nonwhite children is scarce and inadequate, and for the fact that almost one million Africans a year are arrested and gaoled or fined for breaches of innumerable pass and permit laws which do not apply to whites.

I could carry on in this strain, and talk on every facet of South African life from the cradle to the grave. But these facts today are becoming known to all the world. A fierce spotlight of world attention has been thrown on them. Try as our governments and its apologists will, with honeyed words about "separate development" and eventual "independence" in so-called "Bantu homelands," nothing can conceal the reality of South African conditions. I, as a Christian, have always felt that there is one thing above all about "apartheid" or "separate development" that is unforgivable. It seems utterly indifferent to the suffering of individual persons, who lose their land, their homes, their jobs, in the pursuit of what is surely the most terrible dream in the world. This terrible dream is not held onto by a crackpot group on the fringe of society, or by Ku Klux Klansmen, of whom we have a sprinkling. It is the deliberate policy of a government, supported actively by a large part of the white population, and tolerated passively by an overwhelming white majority, but now fortunately rejected by an encouraging white minority who have thrown their lot with nonwhites who are overwhelmingly opposed to so-called separate development.

Thus it is that the golden age of Africa's independence is also the dark age of South Africa's decline and retrogression, brought about by men who, when revolutionary changes that entrenched fundamental human rights were taking place in Europe, were closed in on the tip of South Africa—and so missed the wind of progressive change.

In the wake of that decline and retrogression, bitterness between men grows to alarming heights; the economy declines as confidence ebbs away; unemployment rises; government becomes increasingly dictatorial and intolerant of constitutional and legal procedures, increasingly violent and suppressive; there is a constant drive for more policemen, more soldiers, more armaments, banishments without trial and penal whippings. All the trappings of medieval backwardness and cruelty come to the fore. Education is being reduced to an instrument of subtle indoctrination, slanted and biased reporting in the organs of public information, a creeping censorship, book-banning and blacklisting, all these, spread their shadows over the land. This is South Africa today, in the age of Africa's greatness.

But beneath the surface there is a spirit of defiance. The people of South Africa have never been a docile lot, least of all the African people. We have a long tradition of struggle for our national rights, reaching back to the very beginnings of white settlement and conquest 300 years ago. Our history is one of opposition to domination, of protest and refusal to submit to tyranny. Consider some of our great names; the great warrior and nation-builder Shaka, who welded tribes together into the Zulu nation from which I spring; Moshoeshoe, the statesman and nation-builder who fathered the Basuto nation and placed Basutoland beyond the reach of the claws of the South African whites; Hintsa of the Xhosas who chose death rather than surrender his territory to white invaders. All these and other royal names, as well as other great chieftains, resisted manfully white intrusion. Consider also the sturdiness of the stock that nurtured the foregoing great names. I refer to our forebears, who in trekking from the north to the southernmost tip of Africa centuries ago braved rivers that are perennially swollen; hacked their way through treacherous jungle and forest; survived the plagues of the then untamed lethal diseases of a multifarious nature that abounded in Equatorial Africa and wrested themselves from the gaping mouths of the beasts of prey. They endured it all. They settled in these parts of Africa to build a future worthwhile for us their offspring. Whilst the social and political conditions have changed and the problems we face are different, we too, their progeny, find ourselves facing a situation where we have to struggle for our very survival as human beings. Although methods of struggle may differ from time to time, the universal human strivings for liberty remain unchanged. We, in our situation have chosen the path of nonviolence of our own volition. Along this path we have organized many heroic campaigns. All the strength of progressive leadership in South Africa, all my life and strength has been given to the pursuance of this method, in an attempt to avert disaster in the interests of South Africa, and have bravely paid the penalties for it.

It may well be that South Africa's social system is a monument to racialism and race oppression, but its people are the living testimony to the unconquerable spirit of mankind. Down the years, against seemingly overwhelming odds, they have sought the goal of fuller life and liberty, striving with incredible determination and fortitude for the right to live as men— free men. In this, our country is not unique. Your recent and inspiring history, when the Axis Powers overran most European States, is testimony of this unconquerable spirit of mankind. People of Europe formed Resistance Movements that finally helped to break the power of the combination of Nazism and Fascism with their creed of race arrogance and herrenvolk mentality.

Every people have, at one time or another in their history, been plunged into such struggle. But generally the passing of time has seen the barriers of freedom going down, one by one. Not so in South Africa. Here the barriers do not go down. Each step we take forward, every achievement we chalk up, is cancelled out by the raising of new and higher barriers to our advance. The colour bars do not get weaker; they get stronger. The bitterness of the struggle mounts as liberty comes step by step closer to the freedom fighter's grasp. All too often, the protests and demonstrations of our people have been beaten back by force; but they have never been silenced.

Through all this cruel treatment in the name of law and order, our people, with a few exceptions, have remained nonviolent. If today this peace Award is given to South Africa through a black man, it is not because we in South Africa have won our fight for peace and human brotherhood. Far from it. Perhaps we stand farther from victory than any other people in Africa. But nothing which we have suffered at the hands of the government has turned us from our chosen path of disciplined resistance. It is for this, I believe, that this Award is given.

How easy it would have been in South Africa for the natural feelings of resentment at white domination to have been turned into feelings of hatred and a desire for revenge against the white community. Here, where every day in every aspect of life, every nonwhite comes up against the ubiquitous sign, "Europeans Only," and the equally ubiquitous policeman to enforce it—here it could well be expected that a racialism equal to that of their oppressors would flourish to counter the white arrogance towards blacks. That it has not done so is no accident. It is because, deliberately and advisedly, African leadership for the past 50 years, with the inspiration of the African National Congress, which I had the honour to lead for the last decade or so until it was banned, had set itself steadfastly against racial vaingloriousness. We know that in so doing we passed up opportunities for an easy demogogic appeal to the natural passions of a people denied freedom and liberty; we discarded the chance of an easy and expedient emotional appeal. Our vision has always been that of a non-racial democratic South Africa which upholds the rights of all who live in our country to remain there as full citizens with equal rights and responsibilities with all others. For the consummation of this ideal we have laboured unflinchingly. We shall continue to labour unflinchingly.

It is this vision which prompted the African National Congress to invite members of other racial groups who believe with us in the brotherhood of man and in the freedom of all people to join with us in establishing a non-racial democratic South Africa. Thus the African National Congress in its day brought about the Congress Alliance and welcomed the emergence of the Liberal Party and the Progressive Party, who to an encouraging measure support these ideals.

The true patriots of South Africa, for whom I speak, will be satisfied with nothing less than the fullest democratic rights. In government we will not be satisfied with anything less than direct individual adult suffrage and the right to stand for and be elected to all organs of government. In economic matters we will be satisfied with nothing less than equality of opportunity in every sphere, and the enjoyment by all of those heritages which form the resources of the country which up to now have been appropriated on a racial "whites only" basis. In culture we will be satisfied with nothing less than the opening of all doors of learning to nonsegregatory institutions on the sole criterion of ability. In the social sphere we will be satisfied with nothing less than the abolition of all racial bars. We do not demand these things for people of African descent alone. We demand them for all South Africans, white and black. On these principles we are uncompromising. To compromise would be an expediency that is most treacherous to democracy, for in the turn of events the sweets of economic, political and social privileges that are a monopoly of only one section of a community turn sour even in the mouths of those who eat them. Thus apartheid in practice is proving to be a monster created by Frankenstein. That is the tragedy of the South African scene.

Many spurious slogans have been invented in our country in an effort to redeem uneasy race relations—"trusteeship," "separate development," "race federation" and elsewhere "partnership." These are efforts to sidetrack us from the democratic road, mean delaying tactics that fool no one but the unwary. No euphemistic naming will ever hide their hideous nature. We reject these policies because they do not measure up to the best mankind has striven for throughout the ages; they do great offence to man's sublime aspirations that have remained true in a sea of flux and change down the ages, aspirations of which the United Nations Declaration of Human Rights is a culmination. This is what we stand for. This is what we fight for.

In their fight for lasting values, there are many things that have sustained the spirit of the freedom-loving people of South Africa and those in the yet unredeemed parts of Africa where the white man claims resolutely proprietary rights over democracy, a universal heritage. High amongst them—the things that have sustained us—stands the magnificent support of the progressive people and governments throughout the world, amongst whom number the people and government of the country of which I am today a guest; our brothers in Africa; especially in the Independent African States; organizations who share the outlook we embrace in countries scattered right across the face of the globe; the United Nations Organization jointly and some of its member nations singly. In their defence of peace in the world through actively upholding the equality of man all these groups have reinforced our undying faith in the unassailable rightness and justness of our cause. To all of them I say: Alone we would have been weak. Our heartfelt appreciation of your acts of support of us, we cannot adequately express, nor can we ever forget; now or in the future when victory is behind us, and South Africa's freedom rests in the hands of all her people.

We South Africans, however, equally understand that much as others might do for us, our freedom cannot come to us as a gift from abroad. Our freedom we must make ourselves. All honest freedom-loving people have dedicated themselves to that task. What we need is the courage that rises with danger.

Whatever may be the future of our freedom efforts, our cause is the cause of the liberation of people who are denied freedom. Only on this basis can the peace of Africa and the world be firmly founded. Our cause is the cause of equality between nations and peoples. Only thus can the brotherhood of man be firmly established. It is encouraging and elating to remind you that despite her humiliation and torment at the hands of white rule, the spirit of Africa in quest for freedom has been, generally, for peaceful means to the utmost.

If I have dwelt at length on my country's race problem, it is not as though other countries on our continent do not labour under these problems, but because it is here in the Republic of South Africa that the race problem is most acute. Perhaps in no other country on the continent is white supremacy asserted with greater vigour and determination and a sense of righteousness. This places the opponents of apartheid in the front rank of those who fight white domination.

In bringing my address to a close, let me invite Africa to cast her eyes beyond the past and to some extent the present with their woes and tribulations, trials and failures, and some successes, and see herself an emerging continent, bursting to freedom through the shell of centuries of serfdom. This is Africa's age—the dawn of her fulfillment, yes, the moment when she must grapple with destiny to reach the summits of sublimity, saying ours was a fight for noble values and worthy ends, and not for lands and the enslavement of man.

Africa is a vital subject matter in the world of today, a focal point of world interest and concern. Could it not be that history has delayed her rebirth for a purpose? The situation confronts her with inescapable challenges, but more importantly with opportunities for service to herself and mankind. She evades the challenges and neglects the opportunites to her shame, if not her doom. How she sees her destiny is a more vital and rewarding quest than bemoaning her past with its humiliations and sufferings.

The address could do no more than pose some questions and leave it to the African leaders and peoples to provide satisfying answers and responses by their concern for higher values and by their noble actions that could be

> . . . footprints on the sands of time;
> Footprints, that perhaps another,
> Sailing o'er life's solemn main,
> A forlorn and shipwrecked brother,
> Seeing, shall take heart again.

Still licking the scars of past wrongs perpetrated on her, could she not be magnanimous and practice no revenge? Her hand of friendship scornfully rejected, her pleas for justice and fair play spurned, should she not nonetheless seek to turn enmity into amity? Though robbed of her lands, her independence and opportunities—this, oddly enough, often in the name of civilization and even Christianity—should she not see her destiny as being that of making a distinctive contribution to human progress and human relationships with a peculiar new African flavour enriched by the diversity of cultures she enjoys, thus building on the summits of present human achievement an edifice that would be one of the finest tributes to the genius of man?

She should see this hour of her fulfillment as a challenge to her to labour on until she is purged of racial domination, and as an opportunity of reassuring the world that her national aspiration lies, not in overthrowing white domination to replace it by a black caste, but in building a non-racial democracy that shall be a monumental brotherhood, a "brotherly community" with none discriminated against on grounds of race or colour.

What of the many pressing and complex political, economic and cultural problems attendant upon the early years of a newly independent state? These, and others which are the legacy of colonial days, will tax to the limit the statesmanship, ingenuity, altruism and steadfastness of African leadership and its unbending avowal to democratic tenets in statecraft. To us all, free or not free, the call of the hour is to redeem the name and honour of Mother Africa.

In a strife-torn world, tottering on the brink of complete destruction by man-made nuclear weapons, a free and independent Africa is in the making, in answer to the injunction and challenge of history: "Arise and shine for thy light is come." Acting in concert with other nations, she is man's last hope for a mediator between East and West, and is qualified to demand of the great powers to "turn the swords into ploughshares" because two-thirds of mankind is hungry and illiterate; to engage human energy, human skill and human talent in the service of peace, for the alternative is unthinkable—war, destruction and desolation; and to build a world community which will stand as a lasting monument to the millions of men and women, to such devoted and distinguished world citizens and fighters for peace as the late Dag Hammarskjold, who have given their lives that we may live in happiness and peace.

Africa's qualification for this noble task is incontestable, for her own fight has never been and is not now a fight for conquest of land, for accumulation of wealth or domination of peoples, but for the recognition and preservation of the rights of man and the establishment of a truly free world for a free people.

APPENDIX III

The Speech by Premier Patrice Lumumba
on Independence Day

June 30, 1960

Ladies and gentlemen of the Congo who have fought for the independence won today, I salute you in the name of the Congolese government.

To all of you, my friends who have struggled continuously on our side, I ask you to make this day, June 30, 1960, an illustrious date which you will keep indelibly engraved in your hearts—a date of which you will proudly teach your children the significance so that they in their turn may make known to their sons and grandsons the glorious history of our struggle for freedom.

Because this independence of the Congo, (sic) as it is proclaimed today in agreement with Belgium—the friendly country with whom we stand on equal terms—no Congolese worthy of the name will ever forget that independence has been won by struggle, an everyday struggle, an intense and idealistic struggle, a struggle in which we have spared neither our forces, our privations, our suffering, nor our blood.

This struggle of tears, fire, and blood makes us profoundly proud because it was a noble and just struggle, an indispensable struggle to put an end to the humiliating bondage imposed on us by force.

Our lot was 80 years of colonial rule; our wounds are still too fresh and painful to be driven from our memory.

We have known tiring labor exacted in exchange for salary which did not allow us to satisfy our hunger, to clothe and lodge ourselves decently or to raise our children like loved beings.

We have known ironies, insults, blows which we had to endure morning, noon, and night because we were "Negroes." Who will forget that to a Negro the familiar verb forms were used, not indeed as with a friend, but because the honorable formal verb forms were reserved for the whites?

We have known that our lands were despoiled in the name of supposedly legal texts which recognized only the law of the stronger.

We have known that the law was never the same depending on whether it concerned a white or a Negro: accommodating for one group, it was cruel and inhuman for the other.

We have known the atrocious sufferings of those banished for political opinions or religious beliefs; exiled in their own countries, their end was truly worse than death itself.

We have known that there were magnificent houses for the whites in the cities and tumble-down straw huts for the Negroes, that a Negro was not admitted in movie houses or restaurants or stores labeled "European," that a Negro traveled in the hulls of river boats at the feet of the white in his first class cabin.

Who will forget, finally, the fusillades where so many of our brothers perished or the prisons where all those were brutally flung who no longer wished to submit to the regime of a law of oppression and exploitation which the colonists had made a tool of their domination?

All that, my brothers, we have profoundly suffered.

But for all of that, we who by the votes of your elected representatives have been approved to direct our beloved country, we who have suffered the colonial oppression in body and heart, we say to you, all of that is henceforth finished.

The Congo Republic has been proclaimed and our beloved country is now in the hands of its own children.

Together, my brothers, we are going to begin a new struggle, a sublime struggle which is going to lead our country to peace, prosperity, and grandeur.

Together we are going to establish social justice and assure that everyone receives just remuneration for his work.

We are going to show the world what the black man can do when he works in freedom, and we are going to make the Congo the center of radiance for the whole of Africa.

We are going to awaken to what the lands of our beloved country provide her children.

We are going to reexamine all the former laws and from them make new laws which will be noble and just.

We are going to put an end to the oppression of free thought so that all citizens may enjoy fully the fundamental liberties provided for in the declaration of the Rights of Man.

We are going to suppress effectually all discrimination, whatever it may be, and give each person the just place which his human dignity, his work, and his devotion to his country merit him.

We are not going to let a peace of guns and bayonets prevail, but rather a peace of courage and good will.

And for all that, beloved compatriots, rest assured that we will be able to count not only on our enormous forces and our immense riches but also on the assistance of many foreign countries with whom we will accept collaboration so long as it is honest and does not seek to impose any politics whatever.

In this domain, even Belgium who after all understands the meaning of history has not tried to oppose our independence further and is ready to give us her help and her friendship; and a treaty with this understanding has been signed between our two equal and independent countries. This cooperation, I am sure, will be profitable to both countries. While remaining vigilant, we will be able for our part to respect the promises freely given.

Thus, as much at home as abroad, the new Congo which my government is going to create will be a rich, free, and prosperous country. But in order that we may arrive at this goal without delay, I ask all of you, legislators and Congolese citizens to assist me with all your strength.

—I ask all of you to forget the hazardous tribal quarrels which exhaust our strength and make us contemptible to the foreigner.

—I ask the parliamentary minority to help my government with a constructive opposition, and to stay strictly in legal and democratic channels.

—I ask all of you not to retreat in the face of any sacrifice necessary to assure the success of our great undertaking.

—I ask you finally to respect unconditionally the life and well-being of your fellow citizens and of the foreigners settled in our country; if the conduct of these foreigners leaves something to be desired, our courts of justice will be prompt to expel them from the territory of the Republic; if on the other hand their conduct is good, they must be left in peace, because they also work for the prosperity of our country.

The independence of the Congo marks a decisive step toward the liberation of the entire African continent.

There, Lord, Excellencies, Ladies, Gentlemen, my brothers in ancestry, my brothers in struggle, my compatriots, there is what I have wanted to tell you in the name of the government on this magnificent day of our complete and sovereign Independence.

Our government, strong, national, popular, will be the hope of this country.

I invite all Congolese citizens, men, women, and children, to devote themselves resolutely to their work with a view toward creating a national economy and building our economic independence.

> Homage to the Champions of National Liberty!
> Long live African Independence and Unity!
> Long live the Independent and Sovereign Congo!

APPENDIX IV

The one striking exception to the peaceful transition of power from white to black hands in Africa has been the Congo. Since the Congo disorders have had a distinct racial aspect, the advocates of separation of the races have used the Congo situation to document their contention that the black man will not offer the hand of reconciliation to his former white master. In my book *White Man's Future in Black Africa,** I analyze the reasons for the special situation in the Congo in one chapter devoted to that subject. The following appendix is from chapter ten of that book.

FOOTNOTE ON THE CONGO

The situation in the ex-Belgian Congo has been influenced by a variety of complex factors not related to race relations. It is therefore difficult at this early point in the Congo story,

---

* Reprinted by permission of Macfadden Books. Copyright 1962 by Macfadden-Bartell Corp.

which is still highly fluid, to determine what aspects were primarily related to relationships between the blacks and whites. This will indeed be a most interesting facet of the Congo situation to study when the present ordeal is over and one is able to gather and analyze all the facts. Here in this book the author has been forced to content himself with a brief reflection on the racial aspects of the Congo developments as they are now known. This is the reason for entitling these comments "Footnote on the Congo." At a later time when all the facts are available, a full analysis can be given.

Let us begin by briefly reviewing the historical setting.

Belgium's entry into and exit from Congo affairs were accompanied by scandal. Following the Berlin Conference of 1885, the vast area of the Congo came under the control of Belgium's Léopold II. Maintained as an entity separate from Belgium, the territory was administered through the mechanism of the Congo Free State organization.

During the first few decades of Léopold's reign, the unjust treatment of the Congolese reached the point of international controversy. By 1908 the international opposition to Léopold's policies in the Congo was sufficiently strong to bring an end to the King's control. Sovereignty passed into the hands of the Belgium government. Colin Legum sums up the legacy of the King's rule as follows:

"When it came to inviting Africans to a meal, to buying meat at the same butcher's shop, to travelling next to an African in the train, to letting their children sit on the same school benches as young Africans, to the great bitterness of the évolués the Europeans objected. All had been well as long as the Africans had remained as children who were to be taught and encouraged . . . but the limit was reached at the adolescent stage, when Africans began to want to be treated in terms of equality, as adults, to be regarded as brothers rather than sons." [1]

Hard racial distinctions did exist. Although beginning in 1957 the Belgian government undertook a drastic campaign to eliminate all legal discriminations, it was too late to alter the scars. The young men, especially in the urban centers, had benefited from a paternalistic kindness, but were rebuffed when as adult men they sought mature relationships. This happened at a time when their neighbors had freed themselves from any remaining racial discriminations that might have existed and were even participating in their own governments.

This rigid paternalistic system, which until recently was praised by some as the ideal colonialism, was based on a tripartite power structure of state, church and business. To the African this interlocking directorate was "all white," and his relationship to it was like that of the servant to the master. The quick and drastic last-minute changes of the late 1950's did not change this image.

From the moment that the decision for independence was made in February 1960 until the chaotic days began in early July 1960, there was little indication from the Europeans resident in the Congo that they feared any kind of racial struggle. A little reflection by them on Congo history, current events in other parts of Africa and human relations might have prepared them for the post-independence development.

It is also true that many outside observers did not realize that all was not well in regard to race relations. The racial implications in the various incidents against the colonial power in the preceding years were disregarded.

"The Congo was a pitiful land when he took it over; it was more pitiful what he had done with it. Although slavery had finally been put down, forced labor, autocracy and harsher poverty were put in its place.

". . . Léopold had replaced the natives' fear of the slaver with a fear of the white man." [2]

Against this background the Belgian government began their 52 year rule of the Congo, lasting from 1908 to 1960. The first part of this period extended from 1908 to 1957. During these 49 years the government of the Congo was a complete bureaucracy run by a governor-general, with little reservations on his power. The administration was exclusively a Belgian affair. There was no program of Africanization similar to that which the British and French had advanced in their areas. At the time of independence only one African had risen to high public office in the Congo civil service! The leadership programs initiated in 1957 and 1958 hardly had sufficient time to be implemented when the power to govern passed from Belgian to Congo hands.

During this more than half century of stewardship the Belgians prepared the Congolese for everything but self-government. An extensive welfare program was implemented setting up comprehensive health and hospital services, pensions, primary and vocational schools. Colin Legum had another cogent observation summing up this period of Belgian rule.

"Who could deny the importance of these achievements? They stand as a monument to the contribution of Belgian skill and enterprise in Africa. What this impressive superstructure lacked, however, was a foundation on which to rest. The Belgian view had always been that economic development and education are the foundation of political independence . . . it is a false belief . . . ; no enterprise—economic, educational, or religious—can stand unless it is embedded in solid political foundations . . ." [3]

The impact of Ghana's independence in 1957 plus the force of General de Gaulle's promises to the African people in Brazzaville electrified the younger urbanized Congolese peoples. The first elections held in the Belgian Congo took place at the end of 1957 when council members were selected for Elizabethville, Léopoldville and Jadotville. Up to that time there had been no legislature in the Congo.

The Brussels government started in 1958 to make plans for the Congolese to take a more active part in their government. It was of course too late. By January 1959 the discontent of the Congo manifested itself in riots in Léopoldville and in other major cities. Congolese political leaders began to spring up in various parts of the country. With few exceptions all demanded immediate independence.

With a haste that sometimes approached hysteria the Belgians acted to give political rights to the Congolese. The Round Table Conference, meeting in Brussels in early 1960, was attended by 96 Congolese leaders representing the various Congolese parties and factions. In this drastic and sudden turn of events Belgian colonial administrators who had always been "the boss" were now on an even footing with the Congolese. And, furthermore, it was not a matter of whether independence, but when.

All the personalities who were later to play leading roles in the Congo ordeal were there—Lumumba, Kasavubu, Tshombé, Kalonji, Bomboko, Gizenga and Adoula. When the conference ended Belgium agreed to grant independence to the Congo on June 30, 1960.

In the remaining few months the Congo was expected to carry out all the preparations for independence that had taken years in Nigeria, Ghana and Sénégal. Two houses of parliament were elected in the late spring of 1960; a chamber of deputies of 137 members was elected directly and a senate of 84 members chosen by six provincial assemblies.

The party of the late Patrice Lumumba captured 41 seats

in the Chamber. This was sufficient strength to give him the chief government post as Premier. Joseph Kasavubu, leader of the other most powerful political party, became the first President of the Republic.

The months immediately preceding independence were full of conflicting cross currents. In the minds of some observers there was undoubtedly the basic fear that the lack of preparation for independence could result, in this diversified country, in subsequent political turmoil. There were even greater fears —that the paternalistic policy of Belgium had left deep scars and that the future would not immediately erase them. Professor Merriam clearly states the basis for these fears.

"The basic weakness of paternalism was, of course, that it failed to prepare the Congolese for their independence; it failed to give them a sense of belonging to their own country; it failed to instruct them in the Western systems of government which, it was assumed, they would undertake once the fact of independence was established; it failed in race relations; it failed in education; it failed in understanding that decrees are not a substitute for real human relations; it failed because it established patterns of expectations which could not, in wildest dreams, be fulfilled." [4]

The racial aspect of the Belgium-Congo relationship was one of the weakest factors in the Belgian plan. Once the Congolese young men had benefited from Belgian efforts to introduce European forms into Congo life, they reached the point of looking for really mature relations with the Belgians. Here the Congolese found that the warm interest of their tutors suddenly turned to cold separation. Ruth Slade sums up the impasse in her excellent study on this matter.

The late Patrice Lumumba on independence day, June 30, 1960, in the presence of representatives from all over the world forcefully mirrored the racial scars of the Belgian rule. He said:

"Our lot was 80 years of colonial rule; our wounds are still too fresh and painful to be driven from our memory. . . .

"We have known ironies, insults, blows which we have had to endure morning, noon and night because we were 'Negroes.' . . .

"We have known that the law was never the same depending on whether it concerned a white or a Negro. . . .

"We have known that there were magnificent houses for the whites in the cities and tumble-down huts for the Negroes." [5]

The racial bitterness that permeated the Premier's address was for the most part ignored. Within a few days the already restive nation was to begin the ordeal which still has not ended.

APPENDIX V

In a significant statement entitled "Ecclesiam Suam," Pope Paul VI, on August 10, 1964 in his first encyclical letter, proclaimed the commitment of Catholicism to dialogue with Jews, Moslems and the "followers of the great Afro-Asiatic religions" in seeking the "common ideals of religious liberty, human brotherhood, good culture, social welfare and civil liberty." Not only did the Pope pay a high compliment to non-Christian religions but he also expressed the hope that ideological systems denying God "may one day be able to enter into a more positive dialogue with the Church."

The papal document is a refreshing statement of Christian enthusiasm for the sunrise that awaits man as he approaches the twenty-first century. What a challenge for the leaders of all the races to inspire their peoples to embrace dialogue and to love all rather than to follow the anti-human doctrines of apartheid and segregation. As Pope Paul said, once dialogue has been established between Christians, Jews, Moslems and

the members of the "great Afro-Asiatic religions" man can then
look forward to a "more positive dialogue" between the believing man and the atheist.

Following are pertinent excerpts from the Encyclical.

DIALOGUE WITH THE WORLD

The Church should enter into dialogue with the world in
which it exists and labors. The Church has something to say:
the Church has a message to deliver; the Church has a communication to offer. . . .

Even before converting the world, nay, in order to convert
it, we must meet the world and talk to it. . . .

This type of relationship indicates a proposal of courteous
esteem, of understanding and of goodness on the part of the
one who inaugurates the dialogue. It excludes the a priori con-
demnation, the offensive and time-worn polemic, the emptiness
of useless conversation. . . .

Hence, the dialogue supposes that we possess a state of mind
which we intend to communicate to others and to foster in all
our neighbors: the state of mind of one who feels within himself the burden of the apostolic mandate, of one who realizes
that he can no longer separate his own salvation from the
endeavor to save others, of one who strives constantly to put
the message of which he is custodian into the mainstream of
human discourse.

The spirit of dialogue is friendship and, even more, is service. All this we must remember and strive to put into practice
according to the example and commandment that Christ left
to us.

But the danger remains. The apostle's art is a risky one. The
desire to come together as brothers must not lead to a watering
down or subtracting from the truth. Our dialogue must not

weaken our attachment to our faith. In our apostolate we cannot make vague compromises about the principles of faith and action on which our profession of Christianity is based.

An immoderate desire to make peace and sink differences at all costs is, fundamentally, a kind of skepticism about the power and content of the word of God which we desire to preach. . . .

Speaking in general on the role of partner in dialogue, a role which the Catholic Church must take up with renewed fervor today, we should like merely to observe that the Church must be ever ready to carry on the dialogue with all men of good will, within and without its own sphere. . . .

Sometimes, too, the atheist is spurred on by noble sentiments and by impatience with the mediocrity and self-seeking of so many contemporary social settings. He knows well how to borrow from our gospel modes and expressions of solidarity and human compassion. Shall we not be able to lead him back one day to the Christian source of such manifestations of moral worth?

Accordingly, bearing in mind the words of our predecessor of venerable memory, Pope John XXIII, in his encyclical "Pacem in Terris" to the effect that the doctrines of such movements, once elaborated and defined, remain always the same, whereas the movements themselves cannot help but evolve and undergo changes, even of a profound nature, we do not despair that they may one day be able to enter into a more positive dialogue with the Church than the present one which we now of necessity deplore and lament.

OUR GAZE

But we cannot turn our gaze away from the contemporary world without expressing a cherished desire, namely that our intention of developing and perfecting our dialogue in the varied and changing facets which it presents, may assist the cause of peace between men, by providing a method which seeks to order human relationships in the sublime light of the language of reason and sincerity, and by making a contribution of experience and wisdom which can stir up all men to the consideration of the supreme values. . . .

Then we see another circle around us.

This, too, is vast in its extent, yet it is not so far away from us. It is made up of the men who above all adore the one, supreme God Whom we too adore.

We refer to the children, worthy of our affection and respect, of the Hebrew people, faithful to the religion which we call that of the Old Testament.

Then to the adorers of God according to the conception of monotheism, the Moslem religion especially, deserving of our admiration for all that is true and good in their worship of God. And also to the followers of the great Afro-Asiatic religions.

NOTES

CHAPTER I—SHARPEVILLE AND THE CONGO

[1] Eyewitness report by Humphrey Tyler, editor of *Drum,* quoted in *Africa Today,* May 1960.

[2] Edward Roux, *Time Longer Than Rope,* University of Wisconsin Press, Madison, Wisconsin, 1964, p. 121.

CHAPTER II—THE CRUEL ACCIDENT OF COLOR

[1] Léon Joseph Cardinal Suenens, statement made on May 13, 1963, at the Annual Conference on Non-Governmental Organizations of the UN.

[2] Juan Comas, "Racial Myths," UNESCO series on *The Race Question in Modern Science,* Paris, 1958, p. 17.

[3] G. M. Morant, "The Significance of Racial Differences," UNESCO series on *The Race Question in Modern Science,* Paris, 1958, p. 47.

[4] Vera Micheles Dean, *The Nature of the Non-Western World,* Mentor Books, New York, 1963, p. 255.

[5] Barbara Ward, "We May Be Rich But They Are Happy," *The New York Times Magazine,* May 5, 1963, p. 22.

[6] See Appendix IV for a thorough discussion of the special complications of the former Belgian Congo.

189

CHAPTER III—THE OBVIOUS CHOICE

[1] Rabindranath Tagore, *Nationalism,* The Macmillan Company, New York, 1917, pp. 24–25.

[2] Daniel P. Mannix, in collaboration with Malcolm Cowley, *Black Cargoes—A History of the Atlantic Slave Trade: 1518–1865,* The Viking Press, 1962, vii, ix–x.

[3] Pierre Ryckmans, "Belgian Colonialism," *Africa,* Phillip W. Quigg (Ed.), Frederick A. Praeger, New York, 1964, pp. 76–77.

[4] Margery Perham, *The Colonial Reckoning,* Alfred A. Knopf, New York, 1961, p. 129.

[5] Rupert Emerson, "Colonialism Yesterday and Today," *New Nations in a Divided World,* Kurt London (Ed.), Frederick A. Praeger, New York, 1963, p. 12.

CHAPTER IV—THE EMERGENCE OF THE REVOLUTION

[1] "The Future Growth of World Population," UN Publication No. 1958, XIII 2.

CHAPTER V—DECLINE AND ADJUSTMENT OF WHITE POWER

[1] Arnold J. Toynbee, "Africa: Birth of a Continent," *Saturday Review,* December 5, 1964.

[2] Vera Micheles Dean, *The Nature of the Non-Western World,* Mentor Books, New York, 1963, p. 14.

CHAPTER VI—TRIPARTITE POWER STRUCTURE

[1] Tanganyika and Zanzibar formed one state in April 1964 and are now called Tanzania.

CHAPTER VII—THE BATTLE FOR AFRICA AND ASIA

[1] Douglas Hyde, "Communism in Asia," *The Sword of the Spirit,* Hinsley House, London, pp. 7–8.

[2] Mario Rossi, *The Third World,* Funk & Wagnalls Company, New York, 1963, pp. 55–56.

CHAPTER IX—PHILOSOPHIES OF HATE

[1] Hannah Arendt, *Eichmann in Jerusalem,* The Viking Press, New York, 1963, p. 101.
[2] David Wdowinski, *And We Are Not Saved,* Philosophical Library, New York, 1963, p. 69.
[3] Edward Roux, *Time Longer Than Rope,* University of Wisconsin Press, Madison, Wisconsin, 1964, pp. 115–116.
[4] Fred Majdalaney, *State of Emergency,* Longmans, Green and Co., Ltd., London, 1962, p. 124.

CHAPTER X—PHILOSOPHIES OF HOPE

[1] F. S. C. Northrop, *The Meeting of East and West,* The Macmillan Company, New York, 1960, p. 496.
[2] Robert I. Crane, "India," *Asia in the Modern World,* Helen G. Matthew (Ed.), Mentor Books, New York, 1963, p. 165.
[3] G. P. Malalasekera and K. N. Jayatilleke, "Buddhism and the Race Question," UNESCO series on *The Race Question in Modern Science,* Paris, 1958, pp. 72–73.
[4] Morroe Berger, *The Arab World Today,* Doubleday Anchor Books, New York, 1964, p. 24.

CHAPTER XII—AN OPEN MIND IN ASIA AND AFRICA

[1] Daniel Bell, *The End of Ideology,* Collier Books, New York, 1961, p. 393.
[2] Tom J. Mboya, "The Party System and Democracy in Africa," *Africa,* Philip W. Quigg (Ed.), Frederick A. Praeger, New York, 1964, pp. 333–334.

CHAPTER XIII—THE CHALLENGE AND THE RESPONSE

[1] Juan Comas, "Racial Myths," UNESCO series on *The Race Question in Modern Science,* Paris, 1958, p. 48.

APPENDIX IV

[1] Colin Legum, *Congo Disaster,* Penguin Books, Baltimore, Maryland, 1961, p. 35.

[2] Ruth Slade, *The Belgian Congo,* Oxford University Press, London, 1960, pp. 11–12.

[3] Legum, *op. cit.,* p. 41.

[4] Allen P. Merriam, *Congo: Background of Conflict,* Northwestern University Press, Evanston, Illinois, 1961, p. 51.

[5] For the full text of this address, see Appendix III.

BOOKS AND ARTICLES
RECOMMENDED FOR
ADDITIONAL READING

The following books and articles are recommended by the author as additional background reading on the subject matters indicated.

Man Confronts Man
One Civilization Faces Another Civilization

Lecomte du Noüy, Pierre. *Human Destiny*. New York: The New American Library, 1949

Mead, Margaret. "The Underdeveloped and the Overdeveloped." *Foreign Affairs,* October 1962

Northrop, F. S. C. *The Meeting of East and West*. New York: The Macmillan Company, 1960

Toynbee, Arnold J. "Is a 'Race War' Shaping Up?" *The New York Times Magazine,* September 29, 1963

Ward, Barbara. *The Rich Nations and the Poor Nations*. New York: W. W. Norton and Company, 1962

Rise to Power of the Peoples of Color
Decline of White Power
Tripartite Power Structure

Anand, R. P. "Role of the 'New' Asian African Countries in the Present International Legal Order." *American Journal of International Law,* April 1962

Bigelow, Donald N., and Legsters, Lyman H. "The Non-Western World in Higher Education." *The Annals,* Vol. 356, November 1964

Brzezinski, Zbigniew, and Huntington, Samuel P. *Political Power: USA/USSR.* New York: The Viking Press, 1964

Claude, Iris L., Jr. "The Management of Power in the Changing United Nations." *International Organization,* Spring 1961

Cruse, Harold W. "Negro Nationalism's New Wave." *New Leader,* March 19, 1962

Dean, Vera Micheles. *Builders of Emerging Nations.* New York: Holt, Rinehart and Winston, 1961

Eichelberger, Clark M. "The Role of the United Nations in the East-West Dispute." *Annals of the American Academy of Political and Social Science,* July 1961

Emerson, Ruppert. *From Empire to Nation.* Cambridge, Mass.: Harvard University Press, 1962

Gheddo, P. *Le Reveil des Peuples de Couleur.* Paris: Les Editions du Centurion, 1957

Halpern, Manfred. *The Politics of Social Change in the Middle East and North Africa.* Princeton: Princeton University Press, 1963

Kaplan, Morton A. (Ed.) *The Revolution in World Politics.* New York: John Wiley and Sons, 1962

Kohn, Hans. *The Age of Nationalism: The First Era of Global History.* New York: Harper and Row, 1962

Lacouture, J., and Baumier, J. *Le Poids du Tiers Monde.* Paris: B. Arthaud, 1962

Langer, William L. "Farewell to Empire." *Foreign Affairs,* October 1962

Lensen, George A. *The World Beyond Europe.* Boston: Houghton Mifflin Company, 1960

Mac Kay, Vernon. *Africa in World Politics.* New York: Harper and Row, 1963

Melady, Thomas Patrick. *The White Man's Future in Black Africa.* New York: Macfadden-Bartell, 1962

——— "The Sweep of Nationalism in Africa." *The Annals of the American Academy of Political and Social Science,* July 1964

Perham, Margery. *The Colonial Reckoning.* New York: Alfred A. Knopf, 1961

Rossi, Mario. *The Third World.* New York: Funk and Wagnalls, 1963

Roux, Edward. *Time Longer Than Rope*. Madison, Wisconsin: University of Wisconsin Press, 1964

Silvert, K. H. (Ed.) *Expectant Peoples Nationalism and Development*. New York: Random House, 1963

Spengler, Oswald. *The Decline of the West*. New York: Alfred A. Knopf, 1962

Stoessinger, John G. *The Might of Nations: World Politics in Our Times*. New York: Random House, 1962

Tagore, Rabindranath. *Nationalism*. New York: The Macmillan Company, 1917

The United Nations Secretary-General: His Role in World Politics. New York: American Association for the United Nations, 1961

Ward, Barbara. *The Interplay of the East and West*. New York: W. W. Norton and Company, 1962

Values of the Peoples of Color

Burtt, E. A. (Ed.) *Teachings of the Compassionate Buddha*. New York: The New American Library, 1955

Conze, Edward. *Buddhism, Its Essence and Development*. New York: Harper and Brothers, 1959

Creel, H. G. *Chinese Thought from Confucius to Mao Tse-tung*. New York: The New American Library, 1960

Dean, Vera Micheles. *The Nature of the Non-Western World*. New York: The New American Library, 1957

Deschamps, H. J. *Les Religions de L'Afrique Noire*. Paris: Presses Universitaires de France, 1960

Fairservis, Walter A., Jr. *The Origins of Oriental Civilization*. New York: The New American Library, 1959

Fischer, Louis. *Gandhi: His Life and Message for the World*. New York: The New American Library, 1964

Hunter, Guy. *The New Societies of Tropical Africa: A Selective Study*. London: Oxford University Press, 1962

Kenyatta, Jomo. *Facing Mount Kenya*. London: Mercury Books, 1961

Kritzeck, James. (Ed.) *Anthology of Islamic Literature*. New York: Holt, Rinehart and Winston, 1963

Levi-Strauss, Claude. "Race and History." *The Race Question in Modern Thought*. Paris: UNESCO, 1961

Malalasekera, G. P., and Jayatilleke, K. N. "Buddhism and the Race Question." *The Race Question in Modern Thought*. Paris: UNESCO, 1958

Martin, Laurence W. (Ed.) *Neutralism and Nonalignment.* New York: Frederick A. Praeger, 1962

Matthew, Helen G. (Ed.) *Asia in the Modern World.* New York: The New American Library, 1963

Morgan, Kenneth W. (Ed.) *The Religion of the Hindus.* New York: The Ronald Press, 1953

Mphahlele, Ezekiel. "The Fabric of African Cultures." *Foreign Affairs,* July 1964

Murdock, George P. *Africa: Its Peoples and Their Cultural History.* New York: McGraw-Hill Book Company, 1959

Pickthall, Mohammed Marmaduke. *The Meaning of the Glorious Koran.* New York: The New American Library, 1953

Prabhavananda, Swami, and Manchester, Frederick. *The Upanishads: Breath of the Eternal.* New York: The New American Library, 1957

Radhakrishnan, S. *Eastern Religions and Western Thought.* New York: Oxford University Press, 1959

Smith, Wilfred Cantwell. *Islam in Modern History.* Princeton: Princeton University Press, 1957

Taylor, George, and Franz, Mitchel. *The Far East in the Modern World.* New York: Holt, Rinehart and Winston, 1956

Ward, Barbara W. (Ed.) *Women in the New Asia: The Changing Social Roles of Men and Women in South and South-East Asia.* New York: Columbia University Press, 1964

Ware, James R. *The Sayings of Confucius.* New York: The New American Library, 1955

Watts, Alan W. *The Way of Zen.* New York: Pantheon Books, Inc., 1957

Zimmer, Heinrich, and Campbell, Joseph. (Eds.) *The Philosophies of India.* New York: World Publishing Company, 1956

Christianity and the Peoples of Color

Ahmann, Mathew. (Ed.) *Race: Challenge to Religion.* Chicago: Henry Regnery, 1963

Churchill, Rhona. *White Man's God.* New York: William Morrow and Company, 1962

Congar, Yves M. J., O. P. "The Catholic Church and the Race Question." *The Race Question in Modern Thought.* Paris: UNESCO, 1961

Lafarge, John, S.J. *The Catholic Viewpoint on Race Relations.* Garden City: Hanover House, 1956

Leibrecht, Walter, and others. *Religion and Culture: Essays in Honor of Paul Tillich.* New York: Harper and Brothers, 1959

Mason, Philip. *Christianity and Race.* New York: St. Martin's Press, 1957

Mendelsohn, Jack. *God, Aliah and Juju.* New York: Thomas Nelson and Sons, 1962

Mosmans, Guy. *L'Église à L'Heure de L'Afrique.* Belgium: Les Etablissements Casterman, 1961

Tchidimbo, Raymond-Marie, *L'Homme Noir Face au Christianisme.* Paris: Editions Presence Africaine, 1963

Race Relations in the United States

Aptheker, Herbert. (Ed.) *The Negro People in the United States.* New York: The Citadel Press, 1963

Baldwin, James. "A Negro Assays the Negro Mood." *The New York Times Magazine,* March 12, 1961

——— *The Fire Next Time.* New York: Dial Press, 1963

Bates, Daisy. *The Long Shadow of Little Rock.* New York: David McKay Company, 1962

Commission on Civil Rights. Volumes I–V. Washington, D.C.: United States Government Printing Office, 1961

Cronon, E. David. *Black Moses: The Story of Marcus Garvey and the Universal Negro Improvement Association.* Madison, Wisconsin: University of Wisconsin Press, 1955

Dadié, Bernard B. *Patron de New York.* Paris: Editions Présence Africaine, 1964

Daniel, Bradford. (Ed.) *Black, White and Gray.* New York: Sheed & Ward, Inc., 1964

Frazier, Franklin E. *Black Bourgeoisie.* New York: Collier Books, 1962

Golden, Harry. *Mr. Kennedy and the Negroes.* New York: World Publishing Company, 1964

Gossett, Thomas F. *Race: The History of an Idea in America.* Dallas: Southern Methodist University Press, 1964

Greenberg, Jack. *Race Relations and American Law.* New York: Columbia University Press, 1959

Handlin, Oscar. *Race and Nationality in American Life.* Boston: Little, Brown and Co., 1957

Harris, Marvin. *Patterns of Race in the Americas.* New York: Walker and Company, 1963

——— *Fire-Bell in the Night.* Boston: Little, Brown and Co., 1964

Hentoff, Nat. *Trouble "Up-South."* New York: Viking Press, 1964

Herskovits, Melville J. *Myth of the Negro Past*. New York: Harper and Brothers, 1941

Issacs, Harold R. *The New World of Negro Americans*. London: Phoenix House, 1964

Johnson, James Weldon. *The Autobiography of an Ex-Colored Man*. New York: Hill and Wang, 1960

Killian, Lewis M., and Grigg, Charles. *Racial Crisis in America: Leadership in Conflict*. Englewood, New Jersey: Prentice-Hall, 1963

King, Martin Luther, Jr. *Why We Can't Wait*. New York: Harper and Row, 1963

Lincoln, Eric C. *The Black Muslims in America*. Boston: Beacon Press, 1961

Lomax, Louis E. *The Negro Revolt*. New York: Harper and Row, 1962

———— *When the Word is Given*. New York: Signet Books, 1963

Mannix, Daniel P., in collaboration with Malcolm Cowley. *Black Cargoes—A History of the Atlantic Slave Trade: 1518-1865*. New York: Viking Press, 1962

Melady, Thomas Patrick. "Today's Opportunity." *America*, November 4, 1961

Moore, Richard B. *The Name "Negro": Its Origins and Its Evil Use*. New York: 1960

Myrdal, Gunnar. *An American Dilemma*. New York: Harper and Brothers, 1944

Redding, Saunders J. *On Being Negro in America*. New York: Bobbs-Merrill, 1962

Richmond, Anthony H. *The Colour Problem*. Baltimore: Penguin Books, 1961

Rose, Arnold M. (Ed.) *Assuring Freedom to the Free*. Detroit: Wayne State University Press, 1963

———— (Spec. Editor) "The Negro Protest." *The Annals*, Vol. 357, January 1965

Rose, Peter I. *They and We: Racial and Ethnic Relations in the United States*. New York: Random House, 1964

Rowan, Carl T. *Go South to Sorrow*. New York: Random House, 1957

Silberman, Charles. *Crisis in Black and White*. New York: Random House, 1964

Silver, James W. *Mississippi: The Closed Society*. New York: Harcourt, Brace and World, 1963

Westin, Alan F. *Freedom Now!* New York: Basic Books, 1964

Wright, Richard. *Black Boy*. New York: Signet Books, 1963
———— *Uncle Tom's Children*. New York: Signet Books, 1963

Capitalism, Communism, Socialism
and the Peoples of Color

Abraham, W. E. *The Mind of Africa*. Chicago: The University of Chicago Press, 1962

Africa Seen by American Negroes. Paris: Editions Présence Africaine, 1958

Afro-Asian People's Solidarity Conference. Cairo, December 26, 1957—January 1, 1958. Moscow: Foreign Language Publishing House, 1958

Almond, Gabriel A., and Coleman, James S. (Eds.) *The Politics of the Developing Areas*. Princeton: Princeton University Press, 1960

Al-Razzaz, Munif. *The Evolution of the Meaning of Nationalism* (translated by Ibrahim Abu-Lughod) Garden City, New York: Doubleday and Company, 1963

Brecher, Michael. "Neutralism: An Analysis." *International Journal*. Summer 1962

Legum, Colin. *Pan-Africanism*. New York: Frederick A. Praeger, 1962

Lewis, William H. (Ed.) *New Forces in Africa: A Symposium*. Washington, D.C.: Public Affairs Press, 1962

Ly, Abdoulaye. *Les Masses Africaines et l'Actuelle Condition Humaine*. Paris: Présence Africaine, 1956

Melady, Thomas Patrick (Ed.) *Kenneth Kaunda of Zambia*. New York: Frederick A. Praeger, 1964

Morgenthau, Ruth S. "African Socialism: Declaration of Ideological Independence." *Africa Report,* May 1963

Power, Paul F. *Gandhi on World Affairs*. Washington, D.C.: Public Affairs Press, 1960

Rivkin, Arnold. "Israel and the Afro-Asian World." *Foreign Affairs*. April 1959

Rosberg, Carl G. "Democracy and the New African States." *St. Anthony's Papers on African Affairs*. 1963
———— *Africa and the World Today*. Summit, N.J.: Laidlaw Brothers, 1962
———— and Friedland, William. (Eds.) *African Socialism*. Stanford, California: Hoover Institution, 1963

Senghor, Léopold-Sédar. *African Socialism*. New York: American Society of African Culture, 1959

———— On African Socialism. New York: Frederick A. Praeger, 1964

Sigmund, Paul E. (Ed.) The Ideologies of the Developing Nations. New York: Frederick A. Praeger, 1962

Silvert, K. H. (Ed.) Expectant Peoples: Nationalism and Development. New York: Random House, 1963

Smythe, Hugh and Mabel. "The New African Leaders." Yale Review. Winter 1962

Staley, Eugene. The Future of Underdeveloped Countries: Political Implications of Economic Development. New York: Frederick A. Praeger, 1961

Touré, Sekou. The Guinean Revolution and Social Progress. Conakry, Guinea: National Printing Press, 1962

Wilcox, Francis. The United Nations and the Nonaligned Nations. New York: Foreign Policy Association, 1962

Woddis, Jack. Africa: The Roots of Revolt. London: Lawrence and Wishart, Ltd., 1960

Racial Prejudices; Causes and Unpleasant Results

Allport, Gordon W. The Nature of Prejudice. Boston: Beacon Press, 1954

Alpenfels, Ethel Josephine. Sense and Nonsense About Race. New York: Friendship Press, 1957

Ashley Montagu, Francis Montague. Man's Most Dangerous Myth: The Fallacy of Race. New York: Columbia University Press, 1942

Barzun, Jacques. Race: A Study in Modern Superstition. New York: Harcourt, Brace and World, 1937

Berry, Brewton. Race Relations: The Interaction of Ethnic and Racial Groups. Boston: Houghton Mifflin Company, 1951

Bibby, Cyril. Race, Prejudice and Education. New York: Frederick A. Praeger, 1960

Boas, Frank. Race, Language, and Culture. New York: The Macmillan Company, 1940

Browne, Robert S. Race Relations in International Affairs. Washington, D.C.: Public Affairs Press, 1961

Bunche, Ralph Johnson. A World View of Race. Washington, D.C.: The Associates in Negro Folk Education, 1936

Claessens, August. Race Prejudice. New York: Random House School Press, 1943

Clark, K. B. Prejudice and Your Child. Boston: Beacon Press, 1963

Clark, K. B. "Skin Color as a Factor in Racial Identification." *Journal of Social Psychology*. February 1940

————, and M. K. "The Development of Self and the Emergence of Racial Identification in Negro Pre-School Children." *Journal of Social Psychology*. Vol. 10, 1939

Comas, Juan. "Racial Myths." *The Race Question in Modern Science*. Paris: UNESCO, 1961

Conant, Melvin. *Race Issues of the World Scene*. Honolulu: University of Hawaii Press, 1955

Crocker, Walter Russel. *The Racial Factor in International Relations*. Canberra: Australian National University, 1956

Du Bois, W. E. B. *Color and Democracy: Colonies and Peace*. New York: Harcourt, Brace and World, 1945

Dunn, L. C. "Race and Biology." *The Race Question in Modern Science*. Paris: UNESCO, 1961

Frazier, E. Franklin. *Race and Culture Contacts in the Modern World*. New York: Alfred A. Knopf, 1957

Goodman, Mary Ellen. *Race Awareness in Young Children*. Cambridge: Addison-Wesley Press, 1952

Huddleston, Trevor. *Naught for Your Comfort*. London: Collins Fontana Books, 1960

Jahoda, Gustav. *White Man*. London: Oxford University Press, 1961

Klineberg, Otto. *Race Differences*. New York: Harper and Brothers, 1935

Lasker, Bruno. *Race Attitudes in Children*. New York: Henry Holt and Company, 1929

Legum, Colin. *Congo Disaster*. Baltimore, Maryland: Penguin Books, 1961

———— and Margaret. *South Africa: Crisis for the West*. New York: Frederick A. Praeger, 1964

Lind, Andrew W. (Ed.) *Race Relations in World Perspective*. Honolulu: University of Hawaii Press, 1955

Mannoni, O. *Prospero and Caliban*. New York: Frederick A. Praeger, 1956

Mason, Philip. *An Essay on Racial Tension*. London: Royal Institute of International Affairs, 1954

———— *Common Sense About Race*. London: V. Gollancz, 1961

———— *Prospero's Magic: Some Thought on Class and Race*. London: Oxford University Press, 1962

Mathews, Basil Joseph. *The Clash of Colour: A Study on the*

Problem of Race. London: United Council for Missionary Education, 1924

Maunier, René. *The Sociology of Colonies.* (2 Vols.) Edited and translated by E. O. Lorimer. London: Routledge and K. Paul, 1949

Merriam, Alan P. *Congo: Background of Conflict.* Evanston, Illinois: Northwestern University Press, 1961

Morant, G. M. "The Significance of Racial Differences." *The Race Question in Modern Science.* Paris: UNESCO, 1958

Muntz, Earl Edward. *Race Contact.* New York: The Century Company, 1927

Rogers, Joel Augustus. *Sex and Race; Negro-Caucasian Mixing in All Ages and All Lands.* New York: J. A. Rogers Publishing, 1941

Slade, Ruth. *The Belgian Congo.* London: Oxford University Press, 1961

Speranza, Gino Charles. *Race or Nation: A Conflict of Divided Loyalties.* Indianapolis: Bobbs-Merrill, 1925

Zollschan, Ignaz. *Racialism Against Civilization.* London: The New Europe Publishing Co., 1942

INDEX

203